Around the World with

Aunt Inez, Etc. Etc.

ARLENE LAWLESS

authorHOUSE®

AuthorHouse™
1663 Liberty Drive
Bloomington, IN 47403
www.authorhouse.com
Phone: 833-262-8899

Published by AuthorHouse   04/19/2021

ISBN: 978-1-6655-2039-3 (sc)
ISBN: 978-1-6655-2061-4 (e)

Library of Congress Control Number: 2021905988

Print information available on the last page.

Any people depicted in stock imagery provided by Getty Images are models,
and such images are being used for illustrative purposes only.
Certain stock imagery © Getty Images.

This book is printed on acid-free paper.

Because of the dynamic nature of the Internet, any web addresses or
links contained in this book may have changed since publication and
may no longer be valid. The views expressed in this work are solely those
of the author and do not necessarily reflect the views of the publisher,
and the publisher hereby disclaims any responsibility for them.

CONTENTS

PART III
China

DEDICATION

Dedicated to my three children, now in Heaven,
Linda, Ruth, and Forrest

ACKNOWLEDGEMENTS

Many thanks to my editor, Wendy Thornton, for her enthusiasm and expertise.

I appreciate the encouragement and typing by my friends, Eunice Knowlton and Betty McDavitt.

My sister, Sue Tennart, has written a series of four children's books during this pandemic and still found time to provide me with transportation and care packages.

I am 94. All of my five brothers and sisters are still living, and they're still cheering me on.

PROLOGUE

In 1973, my daughter, Ruth, married an Air Force man and they were stationed in Taiwan for two years. I promised her I would come see her one year, and Aunt Inez wanted to come with me. Since we were halfway around the world anyway, why not keep on going?

Inez Frowine and Arlene Lawless, 1974

PART I

Around The World

CHAPTER 1

Hawaii

As a young girl, I always loved the song, *Faraway Places*, a song made famous by Bing Crosby in the 1940s. The lyrics included the lines, ***"Going to China or maybe Siam, I just know that I'm longing to see / the faraway places with their strange sounding names / are calling, calling me."*** The words haunted me.

The idea of traveling was an impossible dream. My father worked for the railroad and the only places my mother and I could go were limited by the Erie Pass. Even on those short trips, the conductor acted as though we were criminals, and took his time scowling before he approved our tickets.

As the oldest of six children, I had to work my way through college. I worked three jobs (60 hours a week) in the summer. The war was on and there was no social life anyway. My main job was in a war plant assembling wires for B-27 bombers. I took wires from a pulley overhead, laid them out on a long work bench, and then tied them in strategic places. This was called a harness, and when the planes were built, they could put the wires in as a unit, saving time.

At first, the string cut into my fingers as I tied the knots, but I didn't consider quitting. I used a lot of adhesive tape, and was proud to be part of the war effort. Soon callouses formed and the work wasn't so bad. I worked with a group of college girls, and we quickly out-produced the locals. The time study people eyed us all the time. We were making a lot of money.

The only drawback to this work was that they were loading bombs in the next building over, and there was always the chance we would get blown up. At the slightest sign of trouble in that building next door, a loud alarm would go off, scaring us to death. Then the workers there would be evacuated, streaming out the doors and windows, and sliding down escape slides from the second floor. It was quite exciting, and the adrenaline would be flowing as we went back to work.

German prisoners were housed at the Arsenal, and one day I was asked to drive a truckload of them to another building. I hadn't bothered to learn how to drive, since my family had only one car and gas was rationed. However, I jumped into the truck and prepared to start. I felt sorry for my passengers as they climbed into the back. They looked so pale and young. They were either scared or homesick – probably both. However, they had nothing to fear except my driving.

As we approached the building, I put the brakes on too hard. I could hear them rattling around in the back and muttering, *"Ach du lieber!"*

Additional jobs included waiting on tables and selling shoes. But at last, I graduated, married, had three children, and began to work as a dental hygienist.

Then, suddenly, the "Travel God" decided that Arlene should take a trip. My daughter, Ruth, married an Air Force man, and they were sent to Taiwan. Since she was only 19, and certain to get homesick, I promised I would scrimp and save and come to see her within a year. My Aunt Inez, who was 82 years old, and flat on the couch with arthritis, said she wanted to come along. Naturally, I hesitated. But then, the "Housing God" gave me a boost. Aunt Inez lived on 5th Street in Miami, Florida, and a real estate company wanted her property to build an apartment complex. She bought another house and came out $10,000 ahead on the deal. She said she would pay for the trip if I would make all the arrangements, handle the tickets and luggage, and take care of her during the trip. I jumped at the chance.

While I was on the phone with Aunt Inez, I said I would like to stop in Hawaii and Japan, as I never expected to cross the Pacific again. My daughter, Linda, said, "As long as you're halfway around the world, why not keep on going?"

I jokingly relayed this message to Inez, and she said, "That's a great idea! We'll go around the world!" My husband was watching TV in the den when I broke the news to him. He looked like someone had hit him with a club. This is a guy who wasn't thrilled when I went to JCPenney's. But he couldn't say a word, because Aunt Inez was *his* aunt.

The timing of our trip was perfect. My daughter, Linda, was living at home and going to Akron University. She liked to cook, and she would take care of the house, her dad, and her 16-year-old brother.

The most important thing to do first was to apply for a passport. Since they can take over a month to come through, there was no time to waste. I then consulted my doctor, who recommended a tetanus shot. The weight limit on luggage was 44 pounds, and that meant careful packing. I solved this problem by choosing a black wardrobe. Then I bought a pair of good walking shoes and started walking a couple of miles a day.

Aunt Inez bought a three-wheeled bike and went into training. One day, as she was riding down the street, a motorist called out, "You sure save on gas!"

"Yeah," she shot back, "but it takes a lot of Geritol!" Interest in the trip and exercise had brought her back to life.

We took off from Miami on a Boeing 747. It was designed for 319 passengers, but there were only 50 on board, and we received VIP treatment. I especially remember an elaborate steak dinner. In between admiring the stunning views of Tampa and the Gulf of Mexico, the barren Western lands, Lake Tahoe and the mountains, the passengers around us were visiting with each other. They were curious about us and were interested in our trip. One woman told Aunt Inez to be sure to take the silverware on Japan Airlines. "It's so cute," she said, "they expect you to take it."

Aunt Inez liked to collect "souvenirs," but I disapproved. I told her it was "stealing," but this wasn't the only time the subject came up.

Our visas had been delayed and we were to pick them up at the Japan Airlines ticket desk in Los Angeles. I was very relieved to find them there as promised.

Luckily, a patient of mine from the dental office where I worked, Helen Chima, was part of a family-owned travel bureau. She was a world traveler herself, and knew the ropes. Helen assumed that since Aunt Inez was paying for the trip, she must be wealthy. So she booked us into the finest hotels and made the best travel arrangements available.

To ward off jet lag, we were to stay overnight at the Los Angeles Marina Hotel before flying to Hawaii. We had dinner, and decided to sit in the lounge for a while and listen to the band. A gorgeous mulatto woman was dancing with her boyfriend. She had seriously underestimated the amount of material needed to cover her impressive bosom, and therefore, put on quite a show.

Aunt Inez Immediately fell in love with a big Texan at the next table and engaged him in conversation. Nearby were two other nice-looking men. They said they would ask me to dance, but they were Mormons and it would be a sin. I jokingly replied, "I think watching that woman dance is probably a sin, too."

A fellow came up to our table and asked me to dance. Aunt Inez said, "Go ahead," so I did. When we went out on the dance floor, the man said his job was selling batteries and that he was "ever ready." As soon as his back was turned, we fled. We had miles to go – big plans – and we weren't about to get into any mischief.

The next day, we headed to the airport. Japan Airlines made a striking first impression. Just inside the cabin, four hostesses greeted us with smiles and slight bows. Their stylishly cut black hair framed their lovely round faces. Their uniforms were perfectly tailored navy-blue dresses with matching shoes. On the front of their belts and shoes were round red buckles, symbolizing the "Rising Sun."

"Hmmm," I thought, "someone has spent some time and money creating this picture. There's a lesson to be learned here."

As we settled into the plush seats, cool fresh air with a hint of fragrance circulated in the cabin, along with strains of quiet Oriental music. Feeling cozy and pampered, we were wafted to Honolulu.

Upon arrival, Hawaiians greeted us with aloha's, flowered leis, kisses and music. They were a warm and friendly people, and no matter how many times they repeat this ritual, their welcome is sincere.

Our guide for the three days we were there came for us in his car. He was a retired American, or should I say, "tired American," as he was rather grumpy. He didn't seem to have the personality to be a tour guide.

Aunt Inez didn't help any when she began to complain as soon as we started out. "Where are the flowers? Where is the beautiful foliage?" she whined.

"Inez," I said, "we're barely out of the airport. This is an industrial area."

Soon we were driving along a parkway lined with spectacular trees and flowers. Our guide would slow down or stop to point out particularly beautiful varieties. Aunt Inez kept talking the whole time he was talking. I'm sure he had a set routine which he didn't want interrupted. Finally, he got so exasperated, he politely told her to shut up. She took it better than I expected, and from then on, I was able to hear what he had to say.

However, when he offered to take us to watch the actor Jack Lord filming the TV show, "Hawaii 5-O" (for more money, of course), she did turn him down. I've always regretted missing that.

We were originally booked into the Royal Hawaiian, which is the picturesque pink hotel seen in many pictures of Waikiki Beach. But someone must have greased a palm to get our room and instead we ended up at the Holiday Inn. I was disappointed, as the Royal Hawaiian was the "in" place to stay.

My disappointment melted away when I opened the drapes in our room, and saw a magnificent view of Diamond Head, a famous volcanic cone. I spent much time on the balcony, admiring the mountain and beach. Too much time, as it turned out. On a balcony below and facing our hotel, a young man appeared. Seeing that he had an audience, he took off all his clothes. I quickly went inside and closed the drapes.

But I wasn't going to sit in the dark and miss the view because of an exhibitionist, so when we came in the hotel room later that afternoon, I opened the drapes again. The man below was on his balcony, again. But this time, he was dressed and having a drink with a young woman.

"This won't last," I said sarcastically to myself. At that moment, he whisked her into his room. The timing was so funny, I had to laugh.

Aunt Inez wanted to take a nap, so I left her in the room and went down by the pool to write some postcards. The pool was adjacent to the open lobby, and the wind was so strong that it whistled as it went through. It was then that I learned that trade winds are not gentle breezes. After a few days, I found that the constant blowing air made me tired.

The sheltered area by the pool was a pleasant spot, and there was a three-piece combo playing Hawaiian tunes. As they played, a man stopped to chat. He said he sold sewing machines to the Japanese. I thought he must be a fast talker and was relieved when he left.

The bandleader followed him into the hotel lobby and then reported back to me that the man was OK. He was a guest at the hotel. It turned out that the musician doubled as a house detective. He told me that bad characters were known to pick up lady tourists, act friendly, and then attack and rob them on the last day of the woman's vacation. The crooks often got away with it, because the woman usually had to get back home and couldn't stay around to prosecute.

That story shook me up a little. I didn't want to meet any more characters, so I went to the beauty shop. They assigned me to a Japanese operator, and I thought, "Oh good, I bet she'll make my hair look terrific." Wrong! She didn't have any idea what to do with fine blonde hair. My new hairdo looked so bad the cashier actually laughed when I paid my bill.

But, in those days, a "bad hair day" wasn't the end of the world. I gathered up Aunt Inez and we went to dinner in the hotel dining room. We ordered mahi-mahi, which is a popular fish in Hawaii. It was grilled with a little ginger root, garlic, green onions, and tomatoes. The aroma was enticing, and the taste lived up to the promise of the herbs and spices.

After dinner, there was a floor show presented by a family of Hawaiians who sang and danced. There was no glitter, no sequins, no slick production numbers, just natural native talent, relaxed and happy. This was the real Hawaii. I had never seen men dance the hula, and I was impressed. It was like a gentle war dance, fluid but still unmistakably masculine.

By then, the sewing machine salesman had joined us. I was going on and on about how much I enjoyed the show, but he said he couldn't give it much. Isn't it amazing how different we all are?

The salesman wanted me to go up to his room for a nightcap. I can forgive him for asking, as I did look like a floozy – my hair looked like a big cone of cotton candy. I told him I had to help Aunt Inez get her shoes off. That was the end of that big romance.

Waikiki Beach is lovely, but it looks very much like Miami Beach where Aunt Inez lived, so she eagerly accepted our guide's offer to drive us on a circular tour of the island. The road wound along the coastline. With each curve came another spectacular view of the ocean on our right and the mountains on our left.

The mountains are unusual in that they have deep vertical crevices caused by their birth from erupting volcanoes and erosion. They are covered by lush green foliage, which changes from dark to light when the sun, shining on peaks and valleys, is intercepted by clouds. I found the kaleidoscope effect fascinating.

Our guide didn't tell us about our first stop. He wanted to surprise us, and he succeeded. As we rounded a bend in the road, we saw an exquisite Japanese shrine. The pillars stood in magnificent contrast to the green of the mountains behind them and the landscaping in front. The ornate gold trim and scrollwork glittered in the sunshine. As we entered the shrine, the faint scent of jasmine incense added to the enchantment.

The shrine had few furnishings. We crossed the bare floor, made from planks, and went to a plain wooden altar where we knelt for a brief prayer. Although we didn't discuss it, I knew that we were both praying that Auntie would stay well and be able to finish our great adventure.

The grounds were crisscrossed by canals, bridges, and walkways. Hundreds of large goldfish swam in the canals, and our guide gave us food for them. When the morsels hit the water, the fish went into a frenzy, whipping the water into a froth with their tails. The Japanese are very fond of goldfish. Some of the very large ones were said to be worth thousands of dollars.

Executives in Japan insist that their workers take vacations, and Hawaii is a popular destination, as they hold considerable real estate there. At the shrine, we encountered our first Japanese tour group. Unlike Americans, who scatter in all directions, the Japanese stay very close together, their bodies almost touching. They move in a clump, taking tiny steps and resembling a large bug with many legs.

It's almost impossible to get through these groups, so Auntie and I would try to stay ahead of them or behind them. "Hurry you," we would say, "the Japanese are swarming!"

My sister insists that because the country of Japan is so small, at least a quarter of the population has to go overseas on vacation at any one time to make room. I believe her, because we met people from Japan wherever we went all over the world.

Now, before anyone objects to my remarks, I think it's all right for me to make a little fun of the Japanese, because at the next stop, they had a good laugh on me.

As we left the shrine, we paused to admire a small Japanese garden. Artistically arranged rocks and carefully raked sand surrounded an enormous bronze bell. We gave the bell a little tap for luck, and the deep resounding tone escorted us to the car.

We continued our Circle Tour of Oahu, and arrived at a large resort complex on the far side of the island for lunch. Our guide led us through the spacious lobby to the restaurant, then disappeared to a far corner where the guides and drivers gathered at a large table to eat and chat. A lot of laughter came from that table, and many others like it throughout our trip. The drivers had a great time swapping stories about their passengers.

The hostess asked Aunt Inez and me to wait a few minutes in the lobby until our table was ready. Auntie sat in a soft cushioned chair, and sank lower than she expected. I sat nearby and enjoyed watching the people. A wide variety of nationalities arrived at the reception desk, Chinese, Americans, Europeans, Japanese, and native Hawaiians. It's not unusual for adult Hawaiians to get very large, sometimes close to 300 pounds. They are fond of poi, which is a starchy paste made from the taro root. Despite their size, they walk gracefully, as though they hear their lilting music all the time.

Finally, my attention turned back to Aunt Inez. She looked especially well turned out in a silk print dress, and her good pearl necklace and earrings. Aside from her large turquoise eyes, her hair attracted the most attention. She had been a redhead in her youth, but when she grew older, the red faded and changed into a stunning shade of platinum blonde. The light shining down on her from a tall window nearby created a halo effect and made her look saintly.

Soon the hostess came to get us. Before I could help her, Inez tried twice to lift her body out of that deep chair. On the third try, using a rocking motion, she got halfway up. Her knees shook and her hands supported her entire weight as she desperately gripped the arms of the chair. In this ridiculous position, she announced in a loud voice, *"When you lose the spring in your ass, you're done for."*

The activity in the lobby came to a stop. A shocked silence prevailed, broken only by two teenage girls who giggled nervously.

The hostess and I rescued Aunt Inez from the deep chair and hustled her into the dining room. I soon forgot my embarrassment, as the aroma from the kitchen perked up my appetite.

The waitress explained that the chef was preparing Chinese sole as the special of the day. He sautéed cubes of fish to a light golden brown, then simmered them in a broth of fish stock, garlic, ginger root, green onion, soy sauce, and wine. Ambrosia. Served over rice, it made an outstanding lunch, fragrant and flavorful.

Our guide told us to be sure to see the view from the grounds behind the hotel. After lunch, we walked out and found ourselves on a high cliff looking down on the shoreline. Waves crashed against the rocks, creating a spray that glittered in the sun. On the sheltered side of a stone outcropping, a secluded beach nestled in an arm of land that reached towards the sea.

The trade winds were even stronger than in Honolulu. We could hardly keep our balance. Aunt Inez took one look and asked me to take her back to a bench by the hotel.

Determined to get a picture I went back to the precipice. Ordinarily, I like the afternoon sun for photography, but this scene was exceptional. The noon-time sun seemed to spotlight that beach.

But, what a day to wear a dress. I found that I couldn't hold my skirt down and steady the camera at the same time. As I snapped the shutter, I heard snickering and clicking behind me. The Japanese tourists had gathered; they were ignoring the view, and having a great time laughing at my predicament while taking pictures of my backside!

Red-faced, I gathered up Aunt Inez and fled to the car.

We continued our Circle Tour and arrived at a pineapple plantation. I don't know what I expected, but the pineapple plants surprised me. They looked as though someone had gone through the field and perched a pineapple on top of each bush for the benefit of the tourists. At the small gift shop, we were offered a sample of newly picked fruit. It tasted much fresher and sweeter than anything we could buy at home. Just wonderful! We bought a little to take back to the hotel.

Our last stop was at the memorial at the site of the Pearl Harbor bombing. It appeared startlingly white in the bright sun, sad and quiet. I felt angry for the 100th time that our Navy was so stupid as to anchor all those boats at one time in a vulnerable spot. The big question was: when the Japanese dealt us that devastating blow, why didn't they keep on coming to the United States? Many expected them to, and that explains the fiasco of the Japanese internment camps in California. There was no way of telling when an invasion might come, and who among the Japanese Americans might be subversive.

As we turned to leave, I saw a young Japanese couple standing quietly behind us. Our eyes met, and I will always remember the looks we exchanged. I'm sure my eyes looked sad and theirs did too – all of us conveying sadness and regret.

We arrived back at the hotel after that interesting day. Now it was time to pack up and get a good night's rest. The next day, we were scheduled to fly to Tokyo.

Waikiki

CHAPTER 2

Japan

We took off the next morning on another Japan Airlines plane. We were excited about going to Tokyo, and glad we didn't party the night before. It would be about an 8-hour flight.

Aboard were 300 or so Japanese and a couple of American businessmen. The ambience and service were perfect, as usual, and the film presented was "A Touch of Class." In the story, a married man has an affair, and when the couple managed to get away for a weekend, he sprained his back. The story was about an English couple and the audio was in Japanese. Inez and I couldn't understand a word, but it was a riot watching it and hearing the Japanese voices. My fellow passengers were almost rolling in the aisles, they laughed so hard. Later I found out I could have pushed a button and heard it in English. Maybe it wouldn't have been so funny.

When a meal was served, the stewardesses put on kimonos and they looked adorable. The food came in tiny portions in sectioned, black-lacquered boxes. The rice cakes were wrapped in seaweed, and there were crab cakes, shrimp, and other mysterious things. The food was a little salty, but good. The meal came with silverware and chopsticks. Unfortunately, we couldn't get the silverware out of the tough plastic, so we ate with chopsticks. Since the food came in bite-sized squares, it wasn't that difficult to hold.

There was an orchid on the tray. I didn't know what to do with it, so I put it in my hair. That's when I noticed that the Japanese woman sitting next to me copied everything I did.

When the hostess came to take the tray, she gave a little gasp, but didn't say anything. I didn't realize until we came home six weeks later that Aunt Inez had pilfered the silverware.

The trip was comfortable, in spite of its length, and the plane was kept immaculate the whole way there. (This was in contrast to other overseas flights I've been on, where the cabin and the lavatories were pigsties after 8 hours.)

I asked the young people who sat in front of us, who I assumed were students, if they knew what the temperature was in Tokyo. When they said zero, I almost fainted. But then I realized that by zero, they meant 32 degrees. Even so, that sounded very cold for the land of cherry blossoms.

When we arrived at the airport, Aunt Inez and I and 300 Japanese travelers descended onto the baggage claim area and Customs area all at the same time. The result was bedlam, everyone shouting and running in circles. My first foreign terminal and I had to pick Tokyo! I propped Inez up against the wall and said, "Stay." No doubt, she would have liked to be in the middle of the fray and tell some people off.

Then I learned another new fact. Your guide and driver can't help you until you have cleared Customs. You have to get your own bags from the claim area and shuffle them to the Customs officers and lift them onto the table. Most of the time, someone would help me, and this time the students from the plane came to my rescue.

Our guide, Miss Abe, was watching us from a nearby vantage point. She was a tiny woman, had a sweet voice and was very efficient. In no time, she had the driver put our bags in the car and we were off.

On the drive from the airport, the road resembled the Los Angeles Freeway. What caught my attention were the wooden homes on both sides of the highway. They were very close together, usually two story with a carport attached, but they were not painted. No doubt they were varnished or treated in some way, but to us, they looked unfinished.

We were booked at the Ginza Tokyo Hotel in the middle of the famous Ginza shopping area. The bright neon lights and city noises reminded me of New York's Times Square. As I stood at the hotel desk to register, I felt my body tilt to one side and then back again. I dismissed this as jetlag, but then I saw the look of terror in the clerk's eyes. That's when I realized it was the tremor from an earthquake. Tokyo had been expecting "the big one" for some time, but fortunately for us, it didn't come until several years later.

The bellboy took our bags to our room and bowed three times from the waist when I tipped him. Japanese people are small, and real estate is expensive. So, it didn't surprise me that our room was tiny, resembling a cabin on a ship. The twin beds were about three quarters the size we were used to, and the bathroom fixtures were correspondingly small.

As we quieted down for the night, a Japanese woman in the next room started making noise. Of course, we didn't understand what she said, but she was certainly telling someone off. Aunt Inez and I decided the stories about meek and docile Japanese wives were a bunch of hooey. The woman was still ranting as we dozed off. Auntie and I slept for 10 hours.

The next morning, we had breakfast in the hotel coffee shop and watched out the large windows as people hurried to work. They weren't just walking fast, they were running – young secretaries in high heels and men in business suits, all in a hurry. They couldn't all have been late, although many had to live outside the city to save expenses. I've never heard an explanation about why they were all running.

There were several Japanese businessmen having breakfast in the coffee shop. Although it was cold, they didn't have overcoats. They wore long underwear under their suits, and when they crossed their legs, several inches of pristine white showed over their socks. The underwear also crept out of their shirt collars and suit sleeves. Since everyone looked like that, it wasn't considered odd. This style seemed very sensible, as was their habit of wearing a mask if they had a cold. I've always thought we should issue masks on airplanes in the wintertime.

Also among the throng on the sidewalk were several women wearing the traditional kimonos, and they looked beautiful. I'm glad I saw that in 1974. I doubt that many are seen on the street now. They are saved for formal occasions.

Our guide, Miss Abe, and the driver came to take us on a tour of the city. Aunt Inez was all excited about our first stop, which was the Emperor's Palace. We were let out at an entrance, and we walked a long way on a wide gravel path. Aunt Inez's feet were getting cold, and it was hard for her to walk on the slippery stones. Finally, we came to the gate that led to the grounds of the Palace. We had a glimpse of the Palace from a distance, but no one was allowed to go closer. It was considered an honor to be by the gate. Aunt Inez grumbled all the way on the long walk back.

Next, we visited the Meiji Jinzu Shrine, which is located in the middle of 175 acres, forested by 100,000 trees donated by the people of Japan. The shrine deifies the emperor Meiji (1868-1912) as a Shinto God. The emperor supervised the Westernization and nationalization of modern Japan. The entrance to the shrine was marked by a great curved-top wooden gate 40 feet high, held in place by logs 4 feet in diameter, made of cypress. These logs were over 1,700 years old.

Again, we knelt for a short prayer. As we strolled around the huge but plain interior, we met the two American businessmen who were on our flight! Imagine, running into familiar faces in a city which at that time had a population of 11 million people.

As we were exiting the shrine, a mother arrived to dedicate her baby. They were both elaborately dressed in silk kimonos. The grandmother accompanying them wore all gray, as was the custom. When she saw that we wanted to take a picture, she fussed with the baby, arranging his silks, just like grandmothers everywhere.

We then went up 300 feet in the Tokyo tower for view of the city. The stop made me a little dizzy looking down, but it was a marvelous view, and included the harbor where the Japanese surrendered at the end of World War II.

For lunch, we went to the famous Chinzano Garden Restaurant. Each table had a grill in the center where a young woman cooked chicken, beef, sweet potatoes, mushrooms, green peppers, lotus root, and corn on the cob. The aroma and warmth were wonderful after all that tramping around in the cold. The heated saki thawed us out too, and we had a great time laughing with the cook and our guide.

The dining room was enormous, yet the servers all gathered in a clump. If one went to the other side of the room, the others followed close behind like they were afraid to stand alone. This was the oddest thing, like the Japanese tourists sticking together in Hawaii.

On the way back to the hotel, I noticed that there were people sweeping everywhere. Tokyo is very clean. One man was sweeping in the middle of the expressway, skillfully managing to dodge cars. One woman I saw was sweeping a long flight of stairs. She had wrapped herself in layers of clothing, leaving only her eyes visible. She also wore large gloves. (Fair skin is attractive to the Japanese, and they studiously avoid a suntan.) Girls with baskets on their backs would jump on trains during their brief stops and sweep furiously. Then they jumped off again when the train started up.

While we toured an open-air market, we were still very cold, as we had brought only raincoats. After buying some trinkets to take home, I made a spectacular discovery – a 6-pack of saké, the alcoholic beverage made from rice that is ubiquitous to Japan. We took it back to the hotel. I heated a couple of bottles in hot water in the basin and we drank them. Soon we were warmed up and snug in our beds for the night.

The next morning, we were scheduled to take the Bullet Train to Nikko to see the Toshugo Shrine. I was concerned about getting Inez on the train, as the stops were brief, and there were people who were hired as "pushers" to pack the passengers on quickly. As it turned out, they were gentle with us, and we were soon seated in roomy, clean seats. The bullet train goes about 100 miles an hour, and lurches violently from side to side. Not a bad ride when you're sitting down – like being rocked in a cradle – but standing in a cradle was a different matter.

Soon, Aunt Inez had to use the restroom. Getting up and making our way down the aisle was a chore. We saw a door designated with a picture of a lady in a kimono on it. We went in, only to discover that the facility was just a hole in the floor! Aunt Inez didn't have much bend in her knees, and I had a real job on my hands trying to keep my balance. This was particularly true because I held up her slip and skirt and hung on to two large purses!

With the pitching of the train, it was a miracle that we didn't fall. We were laughing so hard that we were in tears and I'm sure the other passengers could hear us. When we came out, we saw on the other side of the aisle a door that was marked, "American Bathroom." We laughed even harder and the whole car full of Japanese travelers laughed with us.

At the station in Niko, a driver met us holding a sign that read, "Frowine and Rawruss." The Japanese have trouble pronouncing the letter L, so that was the way the driver had heard my name, "Lawless." I thought that was very funny. He put us in the car, which still had water droplets on it from a recent washing. The drivers washed their cars every day. The interior was spotless, with white crocheted doilies on the armrests. I just had to jump out again and take a picture of that sign. The driver looked puzzled, but then patiently put me back in the car.

Then I saw a real picture that I just had to take. A young Japanese mother, with cheeks rosy from the cold, was carrying a baby on her back. What was unusual about the scene was that she wore a large red plaid coat over the baby and herself. What a great idea to keep them both warm! Again, I jumped out of the car to take a picture and the driver patiently helped me back in.

The city of Kyoto is a world away from Tokyo. It was the capital of old Japan between 794 and 1868: the seat of culture and art, palaces and temples, craftsman, poets and emperors. The Kyoto of today is a well-preserved repository of the thousand years that preceded the transfer of power to Tokyo. The city, spared from the bombing in the Pacific war, has an antique look. Many of the streets are broad boulevards, widened as wartime firebreaks.

The approach to the shrine consisted of 80 narrow steps with no handrail. I worried about Aunt Inez, but with our tour guide, Miss Abe, on one side and with me on the other, we managed to get her up there. A walkway led past ornately decorated small pavilions, painstakingly restored, with elaborate paintings that resembled embroidery. Arches and curved roofs were decorated in red and gold, with flowering shrubs filled in between, adding fragrance to the lovely setting.

A sudden stir of activity interrupted our reverie. A Samurai warrior in full battle dress jumped from behind a bush, giving us quite a start. He glowered menacingly and drew his sword. He snarled and growled as he circled us, coming a little too close with his sword for comfort.

I expected him to pause and shake hands, but instead, he stayed in character as he bounded on down the path. Aunt Inez and I looked at each other and said, "What was that?" We almost believed he was real.

The shrine itself consisted of several rooms built of impressive dark wooden beams. There were priests and priestesses lighting candles and going about their rituals. Not wanting to intrude, we stayed very quiet.

The sight of the priests and priestesses moving slowly in the dim candlelight, and the scent of cedar, were almost hypnotic. I experienced a deep sense of peace and felt transported back through the years of history.

A thick log about 8 inches high had been positioned across each doorstep to offer extra security when the door was closed, and also to keep out evil spirits. We had to remove our shoes to enter the shrine, and our feet were cold despite the fact that Miss Abe had brought socks for us to wear over our nylons. After Inez struggled over the high steps a few times, she muttered, "God damn." I had to chuckle to myself as it was so inappropriate in that holy place.

We finished the tour and started back to the bottom of the shrine. I was frightened as we started down that flight of steps. Aunt Inez was a good-sized woman, who had become tired and wobbly. Miss Abe and I were both very small, and I felt that, if she fell, she would take both of us down with her. We took it very slowly and I heaved a great sigh of relief when we safely made it to the waiting car. By this time, Aunt Inez's legs were so numb that our driver had to lift them into the car. Aunt Inez liked that, and she made him lift her legs into the car at all the other stops. "He enjoys doing it," She told me.

On the way back, our driver drove us up a mountain to Lake Chuzenji. There were 24 hairpin turns on the road, some so sharp and steep that the driver had to bring the car almost to a stop to make them. On the roadside, we saw trees with ancient wounds left over from a civil war, a frozen waterfall, and wild monkeys that burrowed underground and lived on roots.

Finally, we were back near the train station at a restaurant in an old hotel. The interior, casually decorated with mismatched tables and chairs, potted plants and cushions, and pillows of varied prints, looked comfortable and inviting. The aroma of curry (one of my favorites) greeted us from the kitchen, and we were soon served an outstanding lunch of soup, chicken curry on rice, poached trout (with the head and tail on), salad, and a custard for dessert. With our sightseeing finished for the day, we could relax and enjoy every bit of it.

While we waited a little longer for the train, news of a Japan Airlines hijacking came on over the television. All the Japanese diners watched intently. Then, even bigger news came on. A Japanese soldier was flying home after hiding out for 30 years in the Philippines after the war. Miss Abe cried when he departed from the plane.

Our train ride back to Tokyo was uneventful, and Miss Abe cried again when we said goodbye. After we came home to the states, I sent her an extra tip, because she really had been a dear.

We then busied ourselves packing for the next leg of our journey, to Taiwan, and our anxiously-awaited reunion with my daughter Ruth.

Mt. Fuji

CHAPTER 3

Taiwan

I couldn't wait for our plane to land in Taipei, Taiwan and for the reunion with my daughter, Ruth. I hadn't seen her since she married her Air Force husband a year earlier, and they had been sent to Tainan, the oldest city in Taiwan, which was at the other end of the island. Now, only a train ride separated us.

The guide we had hired met the plane, but he didn't make a good impression. He seemed nervous and preoccupied, and I didn't quite trust him. He was supposed to put us on the train, but he said he couldn't get tickets for that day, and we'd have to stay overnight in a hotel. Reluctantly, I helped Aunt Inez into the car, and we sped off, not knowing if we were victims of a scam or not.

We soon arrived at the Mandarin hotel, and it appeared to be first class. The picturesque exterior reminded me of a movie set in Bombay. Carved wooden panels decorated the front of the building and the lobby, along with red and gold intricate decorations. A full-sized stuffed elephant graced the lobby, and huge elephant tusks formed the arch that led to the dining room.

I registered at the desk and felt uneasy when the guide rode up in the elevator with us to our room. I became more edgy when he came into the room, although I was trying politely to get rid of him.

I teetered on the rim of panic as he walked over and pulled down the bedspread. Finally, I knew what he wanted. He emptied his briefcase on the white sheet. Out tumbled jade trinkets that he wanted to sell. I could tell at a glance that they were cheaply made and probably were not real jade. However, we told him they were beautiful, bought a few, and sighed with relief when he left.

The next afternoon, the guide came as promised, and put us on the train to Tainan. We took the precaution of having sandwiches made up at the hotel, because we didn't know what kind of food we might get on the five-hour trip. This turned out to be a wise move. On the train, they served weak tea in dirty glasses, and boxes of rice with vegetables. We passed on all of it.

When we boarded the train, a large, stern, female attendant grabbed our bags and threw them into a high overhead rack. As the train traveled through the countryside, we became fascinated by the scenery outside. Peasants in conical hats, sometimes known as rice hats or coolie hats, were up to their knees in water while they weeded the rice. Sometimes, the water was so high it ran into the doorway of their huts.

Each farm had a gravesite built into a nearby hillside. They resembled concrete bunkers and there were generations of bones in each one. I learned later that if they became too full, some of the older bones were actually thrown out.

Most of the work in the rice fields was done by hand. I saw one lone man with a hoe, patiently going down a row in a huge field. Water buffalo and oxen were pulling the plows. In the gathering twilight, the picture seemed surreal.

With the coming of night, and darkness, came a new worry. We had no idea where we were. The station stops were momentary, and the signs that we could make out in the dim light were in Chinese. How would we know when to get off? The attendant had disappeared, and I couldn't even reach the heavy bags.

I saw a man of few seats ahead of us who looked American, so I introduced myself and asked for his help. He said, "Don't worry, I'm getting off in Tainan, too. You get your aunt off the train quickly, and I'll bring your bags." Was I lucky!

Once the train stopped, I followed his instructions and led Aunt Inez off the train. The American had put the bags down outside the train and took off. Now I was stumped! A flight of stairs loomed ahead of us. I could see that they led to a bridge over the tracks, and then another flight led down again. Suddenly, 2 nice-looking young Chinese men grabbed our bags, gave us big smiles, and took off up the steps. I didn't know if they were helping or stealing, but I had to help Inez. About halfway up the stairs, she said, "Follow the bags. I can make it."

I ran on ahead and found the boys waiting for me. They were just doing their good deed for the day. I have to say that this happened several times during our trip. Someone would always come to my aid when they saw me struggling.

I worried that Ruth and Steve, my daughter and son-in-law, wouldn't meet us on time since our schedule had changed. But they had solved that problem by meeting every train that came in from Taipei. What a joyous reunion! After hugs and kisses all around, we loaded our stuff into Steve's $50 Buick convertible. Yes, I said a $50 Buick. It had been handed down by many servicemen and had the scars to prove it. But we were happy to be with our kids and to have transportation.

Taiwan has a tropical climate. It was warm and humid, and we drove with the top down. The streets were dimly lit and quiet. We passed a few bicycles and ancient trucks, and even fewer cars. As we passed an open-air market, Steve slowed down so we could get a look. Small booths, lighted by bare bulbs, lined the street. On sale were cheap plastic shoes, T shirts, and vegetables. We saw live snakes writhing on hooks that clerks would kill and skin for you on order. Behind the booths were outhouses, pigs, and chickens. The odors from these and piles of garbage was a real assault on the nostrils, and we didn't want to explore that area any further.

Ruth and Steve didn't live on base. We arrived at their home in a Chinese neighborhood. Ruth was living there unofficially, with no government protection. The Chinese on the mainland would still fire an occasional shot at Taiwan across the Formosa Straits, but I felt sure they wouldn't dare invade as long as Chiang Kai-shek ruled the island. He had been the leader of the Republic of China since 1928. However, he was getting old, and I prayed daily he would live until Ruth came home to the United States. Every night, when the television went off at about 11 o'clock, they ran a patriotic song and Chiang Kai-shek's picture. In it, he looked very old, and it was always the same picture, so Steve and Ruth thought he might already be dead.

The brick house had a paved area to the street, and a 7-foot security wall. Ruth was an animal lover. We were greeted by three dogs outside and a mother cat and kittens and a tomcat inside. She had taken in the alley cat, and instead of being grateful, he'd become quite arrogant. I won't tell you his name in English, but in Chinese, we called him Ah So! He had a crooked tail, but then, all the cats did – the Chinese children thought it was great fun to stomp on their tails.

Aunt Inez and I each had a bedroom, which was nice after sharing one room on our travels through Hawaii and Japan. We closed our doors at night to keep Ah So out, but he was not deterred. He would simply jump on the doorknob and turn it in one motion, enter, and walk all over us.

The first thing we needed to do was go to the base, get our pictures taken, and get a pass. Young men at the base and their wives in town were friendly and anxious to talk with us. They were homesick for their American families, and Taiwan didn't offer much in the way of diversion.

We were invited to a sergeant's house for dinner. The table was set with two bowls at each place, chopsticks, and forks. His wife had prepared rice, eggs boiled in soy sauce, noodles fried with carrots and pork, Chinese melon and pineapple. I knew my daughter and son-in-law were trying hard to learn the Chinese culture, but we didn't like this man, because Steve knew he was mean to his wife and beat his children. He was a self-ordained minister and, (naughty us), we fled as soon as possible after the meal, before he had a chance to preach to us.

The next day, we had a wonderful time at the local beauty shop.

Steve drove us there in the convertible and when the operators saw us pull up to the curb, they came out to the car to greet us.

As I sat in the chair inside the shop, the stylist put shampoo on my dry hair, and rubbed it into a fluffy lather. She kept rubbing and rubbing until I thought maybe she was waiting for me to tell her to stop. I later learned that a head massage is part of their service. She then took me to a dim back room, to rinse it out. It didn't smell too good back there. Their water was not purified like ours, but merely filtered, and I worried about that. Ruth and Steve bought all their water from the base in huge jugs. We used it sparingly. During our visit, I made it a game to see how little I could use. Once I broke my own record by taking a sponge bath with only one glass of water, period. Of course, I was much smaller then.

But I digress. The operator stated that she thought my hair would look good in a "frip." The stylists all gathered around and took turns putting my hair in rollers, sometimes two or three girls working at once. They liked to hang around and practice their English. Often one stylist would run over and consult a dictionary. One girl corrected my pronunciation of the word "aunt." I told her she was correct that, in Ohio, we have the bad habit of pronouncing the word "ant." When they finished, my hair looked lovely, and including a manicure. The entire bill was only $1.50.

A trip to the beach proved to be unusual and interesting. We drove a few miles and came to a park-like setting which led past a cemetery. I couldn't believe my eyes. Ruth hadn't thought to warn me. Dead cats with ropes around their necks were hanging from the tree branches. "What on earth!" I exclaimed.

Ruth explained, "The Taiwanese believe dead cats keep evil spirits out of the cemetery. That's why I rescued Ah So. I was afraid he would end up here."

The cemetery didn't look anything like we were used to. The bunker-like vaults and various stones were in no particular order, just set in at random. They were close together, with weeds, tall grass, and litter in between. People were sitting on the gravestones, eating or reading, and keeping their ancestors company.

A funeral was in progress. Nearby, a table held a red cloth, bowls, chopsticks, candles, and food, as though the group was having a picnic.

They did not want their picture taken. At any other place, we took pictures at will, but not there. Probably had something to do with their superstition that the camera can capture your soul and disturb spirits.

Later, the beach was warm and sunny, with a pavilion that included lounge chairs and tables. The only indication that there were occasional shots fired from the mainland were the concrete bunkers near the shoreline. They had been built in anticipation of an invasion, but showed signs of neglect, as they were sinking into the sand at odd angles. I found this typical of the Chinese. They are poor builders, and even worse at maintenance.

Ruth and I went into the water and I said to her, "Ruth, in your wildest dreams, did you ever think we'd be swimming together in the Formosa Straits?"

She answered, "No, Mother, I surely didn't."

* * * * *

Ruth had heard about a brass factory nearby, and Steve offered to drive us there. Away from the neighborhood and onto a wider road, we encountered horrendous traffic. Bicycles of all descriptions filled the road, along with two- and three-wheelers. They carried heavy loads – building materials; piles of cardboard boxes; families hanging on including mother, father, and two children; and even bathtubs. Larger and smaller trucks were loaded down, zooming past us. Motorcycles wheeled in an out, narrowly missing pushcarts and ox carts. The whole road was a wild collage of confusion and noise.

Steve said, "I'm very careful about driving because if an accident happens, they blame the American. The Chinese figure Americans are rich and can afford the cost. Also, if anyone was killed, whoever picked him up was responsible for the funeral expenses. Sometimes a body will lay on the road for a day or two."

He had just given us that information and was making a left-hand turn when a motorcyclist hit our left-rear fender and went flying over his handlebars onto the pavement. We were terrified that he was badly hurt, and also terrified that we'd be hit again by the traffic that kept coming at full speed as we were stopped in the middle of the road.

A crowd gathered on the sidewalk, and they didn't look friendly. They glowered and muttered to each other. Little round-faced schoolboys gathered around our car, pressing themselves close enough to laugh at our discomfort.

One helpful Chinese citizen walked over and said, "If you take him to be patched up, it would go better with the police. He gestured toward the cyclist, who was now walking around a little.

Without a moment's hesitation, Ruth put him in a cab and sped off to an aid station. I felt proud of how much she had grown up in just a year.

Aunt Inez kept reassuring Steve, "Don't worry, I'll pay for the accident, I'll pay for the accident." We worried about Ruth, because we didn't know where she went or how long she might be gone (at home, a visit to the emergency room took up to five hours).

We were in for quite a wait, as both the Taiwan police and the MPs from the base had to be called. Fortunately, the MP who came was a friend of Steve's. When he examined the car to see where the motorcycle had hit, he asked, "Which dent is it, Steve?"

This time, they couldn't blame the American driver. The cyclist was clearly in the wrong. They were supposed to ride only in the far-right curb lane and he'd been in the middle of the road.

We managed to survive the traffic, and Ruth finally appeared with the bandaged young man. He had only bruised a hip, and had some minor scrapes, so we all came out lucky.

I was ready to go back to the house and have a glass of wine, but we were only a block from the brass factory, and decided to go on. The place turned out to be just a couple of rooms in a private house, and there were no bargains. After all that!

On the way home, we stopped to watch the woodcarvers make furniture. Young men, working in open garages, carved all day and into the evening, with just a bare bulb for light. Ruth said, "Sometimes when we're out late and pass through here, we see them curled up, sleeping on the tables in the cold with no blankets."

Aunt Inez and I ordered coffee tables and end tables for both of us. Then later, we went back, and Aunt Inez bought a carved bar with a green marble top for my husband, Dave, and a tea table with four small stools for me.

During the two years that Ruth and Steve were there, they also bought a dining set, 2 bedroom sets, and many miscellaneous items. They were allowed to bring back 3 tons of materials to the United States, and they did. I came home from work in Akron a few months later, and found 3 boxcars in my driveway. An inspector had to come and oversee the unpacking to make sure we didn't have any forbidden artifacts or contraband. Luckily, we had a full basement under our three-bedroom home. It was packed full. This was 1975, and when we sold the house in 1991, Ruth and Steve were still retrieving odds and ends.

Our visit was about over. It had been marred by the fact that we were unable to get tickets to Taipei. They wouldn't sell us a round trip ticket when we came.

Steve had gone to the station every day to beg for tickets, and finally, on the day before we were to leave, the authorities issued them. When Steve's mother came to visit, they never did give her a return ticket. Steve had to drive her to Kaohsiung to catch a plane to Taipei.

We went to the beauty shop again to get fixed up for the trip to Hong Kong. One of the girls welcomed Inez with, "Hi, Grandma." The stylists were amazed that a woman her age was traveling. Chinese women dressed in black and grey and looked very old at 50. The young girl said, "My grandma doesn't wear bright dress or wear jewelry or have her hair done." Some music was playing, so Inez did a few dance steps to show off. The stylists were also pleased that we had learned a few words of Chinese – nee how (hello), boo how (bad), ding how (good), and panyo (friend).

The train trip back to Taipei was uneventful. Ruth bade us a brave goodbye, but Steve said that when she returned to the car, she really turned on the waterworks. She had another year to go in that place, and for her, the novelty was wearing off. Later, when she formed a small nursery school for American children, she became happier there.

On the train, we didn't have to worry about making our connections. We learned that the trains ran exactly on time. The engineer might kill himself if there was a serious delay. A nice Chinese lad carried our bags to the cab, which we shared with an American serviceman. He said he was homesick, and that we were the first American women he had talked with in seven months. We had a nice chat over lunch as we waited for our flight.

Aunt Inez and Flower Girl, Taiwan 1974

Mandarin Hotel, 1974

Mandarin Hotel, Taipei

Tainan

CHAPTER 4

Hong Kong

Getting on international flights was always an adventure. Each country had its own way of checking for weapons. As we were standing in line to board the plane, a tall, dark, handsome man suddenly moved up behind us, and introduced himself as Elan. He started a conversation. We were chatting when the announcement came, "Ladies first. Line up on your left, please." Elan laughed when I put my nose up and gave him a mock superior look as we moved ahead.

But we were soon taken down a peg with the next surprise. We were led through a small tent, where Chinese girls frisked us. They were so quick with their tiny hands that it was over before we realized what was happening. Aunt Inez and I were laughing so hard when we came out of the tent that the men in the other line looked totally bewildered.

After we took off and our plane reached its cruising altitude, Elan came back around to chat. We told him we were excited about staying at the Peninsula Hotel, and about having a three-day visit in Hong Kong.

As we neared the landing, he came by again, and said, "Be sure to look out the window at the magnificent view. I never tire of it."

Hong Kong is made up of over 300 islands, and the view below was stunning. Some islands were uninhabited while others were built on every inch with skyscrapers and hotels. Landing the plane was heart stopping, as the tiny landing strip headed straight to the water. I understand they have a new one now that's not so scary.

At the baggage claim and Customs, Elan helped us with our bags until our driver and guide appeared and took over. We thanked him profusely and went on our way. We were driven in a large black Ford with brown leather seats. It was easier for Aunt Inez to get in the front seat, so she rode up there with the driver and I sat in back with the guide. When we stopped in traffic, Elan's car happened to be alongside us. He looked very startled when he saw how we were seated. I could tell by the look on his face that he thought we might be victims of an abduction. I gave him a big smile and a wave to let him know that we were OK.

We arrived at the Peninsula Hotel, which in 1974, was the finest hotel in the world. Gosh, was it impressive! It was situated on a bluff facing Hong Kong Harbor. As Inez and I were driven into the great, circular driveway, we saw the famous fleet of dark green Rolls Royces, polished to perfection, waiting for guests.

A bellboy dressed in white, including the pillbox hat and gloves he wore, ran down the steps to greet us. He took Auntie's hand and gently escorted her through the huge glass and brass doors.

The enormous lobby had a marble aisle that led to a reception desk. Small round tables and chairs filled the sides of the room. Huge marble columns held up the ceiling and a Filipino orchestra played soft music.

I seated Inez in one of the chairs and went to register. As I received the key to our room, I heard a rustle of people passing close behind me. I turned and looked straight into a very large belt buckle. I raised my head to identify this large person, and the entourage moved on.

"Did I just see John Wayne?" I asked the clerk.

"Yes, he's staying here for the premiere of his latest film, 'McQue.'"

For those of you not familiar with this name, John Wayne, also called the Duke, was one of the most famous actors of all time, known particularly for his westerns. When I returned to Inez, she was engaged in conversation with some businessmen at the next table. I told them that I had just seen John Wayne, and Inez was disappointed that she missed him.

Aunt Inez didn't drink much – she could get drunk on her own excitement. This was one of those times. She told the men she was going to meet John Wayne if she had to sleep on the floor outside of his door!

When they saw John Wayne the next day, the businessmen told him what Aunt Inez had said. He laughed and answered, "That hasn't happened to me in a long, long time!"

The next morning, we were in the lobby having breakfast, and John Wayne was sitting nearby. I almost had to tie Inez down to keep her from disturbing his meal. When he walked over to the magazine rack, she eluded my grasp and went over to him.

She said, "Mr. Wayne, I'm 83 and going around the world, and I want to shake your hand."

He took her small hand in his big, rough one, and shook it vigorously. His famous voice echoed throughout the room, "I hope you have a wonderful time!"

As he started to leave, he looked at me with a twinkle in his eye. I think he expected me to jump up and ask for his autograph. But I remained in my chair, drinking my breakfast tea, pretending not to notice him. After all, he didn't affect me, affect me, affect *me*....

The next day, we took a tour of the surrounding territories in Hong Kong. Our guide stopped to show us several large apartment complexes. He explained that Chinese refugees snuck into Hong Kong in a steady stream, and they were housed in those buildings for $20 a month. We saw a strange sight, long bamboo poles sticking out the windows. Shirt sleeves and pant legs were threaded on the polls, and the clothes were hung out to dry in the wind. Every day looks like Flag Day in Hong Kong.

As we stepped out of the car to admire the harbor, a girl about 11 years old approached me. Her baby brother was strapped on her back with heavy strips of cloth. When she held out her hand, I gave her the biggest coin I had, and she gave me the most beautiful look. She gazed at me as if I were a goddess. No one had ever looked at me that way before, and I don't expect anyone will ever look at me that way again. If I've remembered that look for 40 years, you know it was extraordinary.

Initially, I thought perhaps the girl was a recent refugee, and hadn't seen a blonde person before. In Hong Kong, I'd watched my dollars carefully, but hadn't taken the time to learn the amounts of the coins. When I returned to the hotel, I discovered I had given her a $5 coin. No wonder I got the "look!"

Later, we continued our tour of the area. The drive up Victoria Peak winds past lush green landscaping and upscale homes. The most memorable was the pink brick mansion where they filmed the movie, "Love is a Many Splendored Thing." We had an elaborate lunch in the nearby Tower Restaurant with a dizzying view of the skyscrapers and harbor below. We came back down by cable car. It was a steep, fast ride, and I sat in a seat facing backwards. Not so much fun!

The road on the other side of Victoria Peak leads to Repulse Bay. As we rounded the bend, there was a spectacular view of a perfect inlet. A large white wooden hotel stood on the bluff facing the water. A majestic balustrade framed the entrance, and large pots of flowers in bright shades of red, yellow, and purple decorated the sides of the steps. Gentleman all dressed in white played croquet on the front lawn. This was a sudden flashback to England in Victorian times, a delightful surprise.

We continued on to catch a motor launch ride in Aberdeen Harbor. The Bay was very crowded, and it was amazing how the Chinese men and women could maneuver the junks so skillfully. A junk is a Chinese sailing ship. As the ship sailed back and forth swiftly, they managed to miss each other, and more importantly, to miss the larger ships in the harbor.

It's quite different seeing the junks and sampans up close. The sampan was a flat-bottomed boat made from wood that was propelled by oars or long poles or a trolling motor. Whole families lived their entire lives on these small boats. Little children had ropes around their waists and were tethered to the mast, so they wouldn't fall into the water. Women cleaned and hung up wash on the boat. Sometimes a smaller boat was tide alongside to house chickens. Officials struggled constantly to keep the junk communities from growing as the harbor would soon become impassable.

On the way back, our guide took us to Tiger Balm gardens, built by the maker of Tiger Balm, a popular, all-purpose salve. Walls and posts were painted in garish colors – pretty ugly actually – but I wanted a picture. I held onto Aunt Inez constantly for fear she would fall, but for the moment, I stood her in a little grotto, out of the sun, and told her not to move. As I snapped the picture, I heard her moan.

I must confess, at that moment, I had an impure thought. "No matter what she has done to herself, we're halfway around the world, and we're going the rest of the way!"

I rushed over to her. She had stepped one step backwards and caught her heel. Luckily, when she felt herself falling, she simply slid down the wall and sat down. She didn't even have a sprained ankle. Thank God!

Hong Kong is famous for its shopping. One small shop after another lined the streets. A Hindu gentleman came out of one shop, caressed my neck, and said, "I will make a blouse for you," in the most romantic tone of voice. We hurried on.

Because Aunt Inez was interested in finding a pretty tea set, we went into a local shop. As she was still looking around in the shop, a man started to talk to me. He said, "How do you like Hong Kong?"

I replied, "We're having a wonderful time. It's beautiful."

He replied, "It's hell when you live here."

I gave him a sympathetic look, and went to join Aunt Inez. We had been briefed before the trip not to get into any discussions on politics or religion. I wish I could have talked to the man privately to hear what he had to say.

The shopkeepers were anxious to sell, and offered to ship any heavier items to our home. We were directed to jewelry shops where the sellers gave a guaranteed receipt and appraisal. I bought a jade ring for my husband, and he was very pleased with it when I brought it home.

I also bought a gorgeous, black embroidered satin fabric with red and gold threads through it. My daughter, Linda, made an evening jacket out of this material. It is still beautiful today.

We stopped at the border between Hong Kong and China. There was just a thin wire fence with a red sign, similar to the ones you might see on the back of an Amish buggy. I looked over, expecting to see hordes of soldiers marching around, but in the valley below, peasants were quietly tending their crops. I wanted to put my foot beyond the fence so I could say I visited China, but I didn't dare. No Americans were allowed in China in 1974, but I did finally get there in 1984.

We had our farewell dinner on a small ship that serves as a floating restaurant in Hong Kong Harbor. Beautifully decorated with little lights up the rigging and surrounding the portholes, it stood out like a jeweled tiara against the dark water. Delicious aromas floated out to us as we approached by launch – ginger, green onion, garlic, rose oil – promising exotic dishes such as shark fin and bird's nest soup. Competing for attention were the lighted skyscrapers and high rises on both shores around us. There couldn't have been a more stunning place to spend our last evening in Hong Kong.

CHAPTER 5

Bangkok

As we waited to leave Hong Kong, the airport was noisy and crowded. When the attendant called our flight, we were happy to be on our way. We had just stepped out of the terminal when two men rushed towards us, brandishing laser-like wands. We were startled and stood still as they wildly moved them around our bodies, under our arms and between our legs! They left in seconds and we laughed so hard that Inez could barely get on the minibus that was taking us to the plane.

On the bus, a young Oriental couple with a little girl about five years old got up and gave us their seats. They stood in front of us and the child stared and stared. Soon, everyone around us was laughing, and the father said, "She thinks you come from the moon." She had probably never seen two light-haired blue-eyed ladies before.

Japan Airlines again provided us with a comfortable and uneventful flight. Thank goodness for that. It did cross my mind that we were flying over Vietnam and Cambodia. Within no time, we arrived at the cool and quiet Don Mueang International Airport.

Our guide met us at the airport, and we liked him immediately. He told me he would take care of Aunt Inez, and that I should feel free to sightsee and take pictures. The guide was a happy, muscular guy who easily helped Inez into cars and held her arm as we walked.

It was an eighteen-mile drive from the airport to the hotel. As we neared the city, there were many vendors along the road selling elaborate kites. Evidently, kite flying is a popular pastime in Thailand – this made our trip very festive.

We arrived at the Grand Hyatt *Erawan* Hotel. As I mentioned previously, my travel agent in Akron is a friend of mine and a world traveler herself. For our trip, she had booked us into the most famous, colorful, traditional hotels, and this was no exception. Aunt Inez said, "It's the best yet!"

The hotel, constructed in the ornate Thai style, had an imposing winding staircase inside the entrance. Aside from this were comfortable large chairs. All around the lobby, glass display cases or full of expensive objects d'art and jewelry.

Our suite had louvered doors which I always thought were so romantic. We had a small entrance hall, a sitting room, and bedroom. A balcony overlooked the pool and the garden. A small table was set with a fruit bowl and an orchid.

The next morning, we were up early as instructed to get ahead of the morning traffic. Our guide and driver arrived to take us on a tour of the King's Palaces. For safety's sake, the guide had instructed us to wait inside the lobby.

The Kings in Siam would each start building their own palace, but they were so elaborate that they were never finished in one lifetime. Every surface was covered with inlays, precious and semi-precious stones, and intricate carvings. They had a separate palace for every occasion, such as one for changing robes or weddings. I loved the corners of the roofs that curled towards the sky and caught the sunlight with their gold tilt.

The palaces even had an elaborate area to honor their favorite elephants. The elephants were buried there inside the walled area, and life-sized models of them were very impressive.

On the car ride from one palace to another, we crossed a small bridge and there were several people along the banks. I asked our guide what they were looking for, and he said they were panning for gold. Some of the small gold nuggets were pounded into thin leaves, which were stuck on the walls of the palaces and pavilions as a blessing. As we left, a brisk breeze blew up, and hundreds of these leaves sprinkled down on us. We were walking in leaves of gold!

Inez mentioned the movie, "The King and I," which we all loved. This Rodgers and Hammerstein musical, set in the 1860s, depicted the relationship between a British governess and the King of Siam. But the Thai people were not pleased by our mention of this famous movie. To them, their King was a God, and they didn't like him depicted as an ordinary mortal.

Next, we were to visit an object of national veneration. Just north of the royal residence lies the grounds of the Chapel Royale of the Emerald Buddha. This consists of all the ordinary features of a monastery, but no monks lived there. The Emerald Buddha is really one giant piece of jade. It sits on a high altar of gold, and crowds come in to pay respect to the memory of Buddha and His teachings.

By this point, we were so tired we had to sit down. We were allowed to sit on the floor, but only if we made sure our feet were not turned towards the Buddha.

Back at the hotel, Inez wanted to lie down for a while, so I took a little walk through the garden and sat by the pool. Nearby, a tiny Thai lady was peeling a piece of fruit for a very large businessman. This was quite a picture.

A waiter asked if I wanted a drink, but I declined. We felt that we had to be very careful about drinking water or using ice in foreign countries. The waiter was so nice that he brought me a glass of water anyway, and I felt that I had to drink a little. A short time later, I felt a gurgle in my stomach. Immediately, I ate a banana and that night at dinner I ate lots of rice. Since we were going on a morning boat ride the next day, I certainly didn't want any intestinal trouble.

After dinner, I went downstairs to get a paper, and some businessmen in the lounge asked me to have a drink with them. I said I could only have one because I had to go back up to Aunt Inez. They were very entertaining Brits who had come to Thailand on railroad business.

I told them I was on the edge of having an upset stomach. One of them said he had that problem on the plane. The stewardess told him that she didn't want him to leave his seat, and he replied, "My dear, what is the alternative!" I love the way the Brits talk.

During the conversation, they mentioned that they thought American women were very spoiled. As proof, here I was going around the world with my aunt but without my husband.

I said to myself, "They have no idea how hard I worked." In those days, dental hygienists didn't sit down to do their work. They stood beside the patient. I did 14 cleanings a day, plus filling out the charts and developing the X-rays. Every day, I took a bus to work. The buses were crowded, and I usually had to stand halfway home before I got a seat. And then I had to stand and cook supper for my family!

But instead of pointing all this out to them, I just said, "Well, I couldn't have a better chaperone than Aunt Inez, and she is my husband's aunt!"

The next day, we took a boat trip. We drove to the pier and our guide easily lifted Inez onto our private boat. I felt like Cleopatra floating down the river on a private barge, but it was the Chao Phraya River instead of the Nile. It was quiet and early enough for us to see the sunrise reflected in the water.

In Bangkok, rivers and canals are used like streets, much as they were in Vienna. A large boat passed us, and on the bow was a young man wrapped from waist down in a blue and white batik sarong. He was heading out to sea, facing the sun and the breeze. His face reflected such joy of living and contentment that it added to my already happy mood.

We passed exotic temples on the riverbank, their golden domes gleaming in the oblique sun rays, looking like they had been polished for our visit.

As we turned into the Klongs, as the canals are called, we saw log houses built on the water's edge. A wooden pier serves as a front porch. Many of these homes have a small farm in the back. Due to the tropical climate, doors and windows were wide open, and we could see the interiors of polished wood, neat and clean.

Many people were on the pier washing. It seemed they washed all the time —babies, hair, clothes, dishes, and themselves. Because of the heat, they bathed several times a day. Everyone looked like they were still damp from a shower. One woman was brushing her teeth as we passed, and she gave me a big, sudsy smile. Little children played on the decks, and jumped in and out of the water, frolicking around like baby seals. One aged man stood on the end of his dock with folded hands, and bowed and prayed, wishing us God speed.

Suddenly, we were at the Floating Market, in a wide place where the Klongs and the river meet. Small boats of all shapes and sizes were propelled by vendors in coolie hats. They carried a wide variety of items for sale such as straw hats, wood carvings, tools, linens, and fruits and vegetables. There were also boats that went from house to house selling cooked food such as rice with meats and vegetables. Our guide laughingly called them "Moving McDonald's."

It's a good idea to visit the Floating Market in the morning. Throughout the day, garbage, human waste, etc., is dumped into the water. The rising swell of the tides from the ocean acts as a natural flushing system. All is reasonably clean by the next morning.

On one pier, a handler with a small elephant attracted a crowd. Inez wanted to get on the elephant and have her picture taken, but I resisted. A few minutes later, the elephant acted up and almost pushed his trainer into the water. We had a close call there.

On the way back to our hotel, we were amused to see secretaries, all dressed up, speeding to work in their own little motorboat.

That night, we had an early dinner. We wanted to get a good night's sleep as we had a long flight to Greece the next day. Inez was all excited that we were taking the Royal Dutch Airline. She had heard that it was de-luxe!

CHAPTER 6

Greece

The Royal Dutch Airline plane was running late. Twice, airline personnel had lined us up to board, then told us to wait again.

In the boarding area, the crew of the plane milled around. They looked and sounded like a bunch of partygoers after New Year's Eve. Everyone looked rumpled. The stewardesses were matronly-looking in their shirtwaist dresses and wilting corsages.

On the plane, they moved us three times before deciding where we would sit. Luckily, the seat in front of Inez folded down, and she could prop her legs up. This was going to be a long flight. Inez said 15 hours. We crossed several time zones, so I lost track. The conditions made it seem much longer.

A nice gentleman from Greece sat next to me. He was very ill. The clumsy stewardess bumped into every wall and corner with her cart. When she passed him, she would hit the side of his seat, giving him a jolt which reverberated through both our seats. I tried to get some plain crackers for him, but every few hours the stewardesses would turn the lights on and serve us a greasy meat pie.

We landed in New Delhi for refueling, but we were not allowed to exit the plane. Suddenly, a health official jumped on board, and generously sprayed us all with disinfectant. A cloud of it filled the cabin, leaving us all gasping for breath. Then they boarded a whole load of sick people, all of whom looked very worn out.

The flight continued. Luckily, I can always switch myself to neutral, and tolerate these types of things very well. However, the condition of the restrooms deteriorated with every mile. That was hard to ignore.

When we landed in Beirut for refueling, I was a little anxious because there was always trouble in that area. A very stern young soldier got on with his rifle and guarded us during the short stop. Once we were on our way again, we sighed with relief.

We arrived in Greece 2 hours late, and the person who met us was tired and grumpy. Inez called him "pompous." He put us in a taxi for the hotel. I wasn't pleased with that, because I was sure that he had been paid to escort us there himself.

As usual, when traveling with Aunt Inez, we went from the ridiculous to the sublime. It was barely daylight, and we drove past ancient columns and arches, shrouded in the morning misty fog. This was a dream-like drive. Truly you could imagine chariots and horses and people in beautiful flowing togas. It was a magical time that I will always remember. For once, Aunt Inez was speechless!

The clerk at the Saint Georges, one of Athens' finest hotels, stated that we didn't have a room. We were a little late, but I knew my gal in Akron would have covered all the possibilities. After stalling for a while, the clerk did find our room and we went up.

First, we had to learn about the elevator. The elevator had iron gates for doors, and you had to hit them hard to exit as soon as it stopped. We heard about this as we were riding up to our room with a nice couple. He was a football player, and when he hit that door, you could hear it all over the hotel. We had to laugh when we heard that sound during our stay.

In the room, after we put our things down, I wanted to ask about breakfast. I thought it might be easier to run downstairs and ask rather than struggle with the phone and the language. I stepped into the elevator and pushed level 1. When the elevator stopped, I hit the door hard, and quickly stepped out as the door shut behind me. I was in total darkness! Panicked, I turned and pushed any button I could feel in the dark. Finally, the elevator returned, and I learned that the desk was on the ground floor and I had been in the ballroom!

The following morning, we met our guide. She was a lovely woman who taught history. We were glad we didn't get the grumpy man who had met us at the airport.

As I said, the new guide was a history teacher. She gave us a wonderful tour of the city and the museums. Of course, we didn't remember all the facts about those ancient times, but the highlight of the museums was the "Boy on the Dolphin" statue which is one of the most famous sculptures in the world. It was a real treat to see it.

Next, we headed to Monastiraki Square, a colorful place where locals sat on a low stone wall and bright umbrellas lit up the scene, with ornate ancient arches in the background.

Finally, our eagerly awaited day arrived. We were going to the Acropolis! Inez was worried, though. Her sister had been there a few years before and sat at the bottom of the hill, crying because she couldn't make it to the top. Inez was afraid that would happen to her as well.

First, we stopped at a property overlooking the whole area. How wonderful that the Greeks had the foresight to save the entire hill. There wasn't a single commercial kiosk in sight. The overview of the Acropolis was magnificent. You could see some small temples and the amphitheater.

We drove closer and parked. At that time, to get up to the hill, you walked a narrow path of dirt and pebbles. On both sides there were rocks and wild shrubs, just as nature had left them. I took one arm, and the guide took the other, and together we propelled Aunt Inez up the slope. She was stiff as a board! I shook her arm a little and said, "Loosen up, Inie. You're going to make it!" It wasn't that steep a slope. We took our time and made it to the top without any trouble.

A young man was scrambling on the rocks below us, taking our picture. Inez thought $5 for the photo was too much, but I bought the picture anyway and now it is one of my prized possessions (and the cover for my book).

We reached the summit and Inez sat down on a large rock. I walked a few feet closer to the Parthenon. When you think about who might have walked there where you are walking, it was awe-inspiring. The stones were worn round by the thousands of feet that had passed by. I wanted to linger awhile and absorb the aura. That was surely one of the highlights of my life.

(Note: I was fortunate to be back at the Acropolis for my 85th birthday. The hillside had been nicely landscaped, with wide steps and paved pathways. It was thoughtfully done, but I was glad that I saw it in its pristine state and that they had added no commercial attractions.)

Now we went from the sublime to the ridiculous. The dining room of our hotel, with its antiques, flowers, crystal chandeliers, candles and white tablecloths was gorgeous. We dressed for dinner in our long gowns, which were popular then. We found that putting on those evening dresses gave us a lot of attention and we got better service.

As we entered the dining room, a waiter immediately fell in love with me. He bustled around the table, bringing more water, more rolls, etc., while Aunt Inez got annoyed. We ordered a small bottle of wine to celebrate our last night in Athens. The bottle was $6, and I noticed that Aunt Inez complained about the price in her notes. Of course, it wasn't really too much, especially considering that ambiance.

An added surprise was that as it became dark, we had a magnificent view of the Acropolis all lit up with spotlights!

Before our dinner arrived, our waiter brought me a rose. I didn't want to lay it on the table or put it in my water glass, so I stuck it in my cleavage. Whoa! Did that send the wrong message! The waiter danced gaily around the table while we finished dinner.

As we left the dining room, I noticed the waiter following us, and I thought, "Now what do I do?" As we approached our room, we saw the door was wide open and we heard loud talking. The head housekeeper was bawling out the maid because our room was a mess. I hurried in to tell her that we would be leaving the next morning and that we were packing. I guess they understood me, and they left. The good news is that all that noise scared the waiter away.

We finished packing and went to bed. We didn't have any trouble sleeping after the action-packed days that we'd had. Visions of yodelers filled our heads as we anticipated our trip to Switzerland.

Caryatid porch, Acropolis of Athens, Greece

Parthenon

CHAPTER 7

Switzerland

Upon our arrival in Switzerland, our guide met us in Zürich, and drove us to Lucerne. She was about 45, pleasant, but all business. I'm sure she must've been a good guide, as one of her earlier clients was Rose Kennedy. She told us later that we were nice to work with, but Rose Kennedy was not so easy to please.

We checked into the Switzerhoff Hotel which is the grand dame of hotels in Lucerne. Built in 1860 by a private family, it had a wide veranda across the front facing Lake Lucerne. This was a wonderful place to enjoy the view and write postcards.

The lobby was large and ornate, full of antiques, stained glass windows, and crystal chandeliers. The elevator was an elaborate, scrolled iron cage, complete with a red Oriental carpet and velvet seats.

Our room was huge, and the furniture was big as well. Swiss people are taller than average. The bed was over 6 feet long, with a massive carved headboard. Big white fluffy comforters welcomed us, but the bed was so high, we could barely climb in! And the bathroom! We had to laugh at its enormous size, complete with a bathtub with claw style feet.

We dressed in long gowns for dinner, as we did most nights on our trip. We looked very "put together" and found that we got better service when we looked fancy.

Inez and I both fell in love with our waiter. He was handsome, pleasant, and very attentive. He had plenty of time, as there were few guests this early in the spring. He would linger at our table carving our meat or deboning our fish. He made us feel like royals.

Our waiter recommended a show in the evening in a nearby building. A family in Alpine dress played folk music on a wide variety of instruments, as they sang and yodeled. The concert was great fun, and put everyone in a jolly mood.

The entertainers challenged the men in the audience to blow an 8-foot Alpine horn. Many couldn't do it, and they were met with boos. The ones who could do it were met with cheers. On a later trip, my grandson was able to blow the horn, and received great applause.

The highlight of the show was when two men in a cow costume, complete with a bell, came wandering through the club. It was such a fun evening!

The next day, we went shopping. Of course, the big attraction in Switzerland was watches. There were big stores and small stores filled with hundreds and hundreds of watches at all prices. I finally decided on one for each of my daughters. There was also a beautiful selection of jewelry, handbags, scarves, and cameras. The grocery stores were cleverly hidden in the basements, below all those glamorous shops.

The next day was Palm Sunday. I will never forget the sight of well-dressed Swiss ladies pushing expensive prams with their babies immaculately dressed in white. The prams were also lined in pleated white linen and lace.

We went across a covered wooden bridge, the focal point of Lucerne, which was spectacular. It was built in 1333. On the inside walls of the bridge, Heinrich Wagner painted elaborate murals. No cars or dogs were allowed on the bridge, and it was a lovely walk on Palm Sunday. There were great views of the city, from anywhere on the bridge.

Lucerne is the center of Switzerland, geographically and politically. In 1291, three groups formed a confederation named Switzerland. Lucerne joined this confederation in 1332. It is the oldest democracy in the world; it never had a king.

For strategic reasons, the old town wall with nine towers was built in the second half of the 14th century. It is the largest of the remaining fortifications in Switzerland. In 1303, the included water tower also served as a watchtower.

Another "must" when visiting Lucerne is the cable car ride up Mount Pilate. This is the steepest cogwheel railway in the world, going up 7000 feet. As you go up, the railway skims over grass and cows. At the top is a well-planned viewing area with a spectacular panoramic vista of Lucerne. This viewing area is great for taking pictures and enjoying the sunshine.

We were also privileged to see a famous sculpture. The "Lion of Lucerne," a masterpiece of the early 19th century. It is dedicated to the memory of the heroic fight and final defeat of the Swiss Guards in 1792 in Paris. August 10th of that year marked the beginning of the French Revolution, when the Royal Palace, the Tuilenierss, was stormed. King Louie VI ordered the Swiss guard to lay down their arms, and then they were all killed.

The lion, always considered a symbol of courage, served as an example for the artist to demonstrate a fight to the death. In the sculpture, the heart is pierced by a lance, but the lion still holds a protective paw over the shield with the lily coat of arms emblem of the Bourbon Kings. This model was the work of a famous Danish sculptor, Bertel Thorvaldsen (1770-1848).

The niche in the rock wall measures 43 inches, the animal 30 inches. The inscription reads, "To the fidelity and bravery of the Swiss."

Lucerne was just perfect, except for a couple of things that disagreed with me. First, I had a short bout with altitude sickness. This was a very odd feeling – no pain, just sort of tiredness and disorientation. I laid down for a couple of hours, and it went away. I told a friend, and he said, "Oh, you should have gone down to the desk. They have oxygen there all the time. That's all you needed!"

I had the same feeling when we went to the casino. The casino was beautifully decorated in red and had mirrors in all directions. These mirrors drove me crazy, and I couldn't wait to get out of there.

The day we drove up to Grindenwald Mountain was a beautiful sunny day. Our driver didn't want to take us over 12,000 feet, because Aunt Inez was 83 years old, and we had to be careful about altitude sickness.

Our guide was a good driver, and he took all the winding curves comfortably. At every turn there was a beautiful chalet with overflowing window boxes. The Swiss have hard winters, and they go all out with the Flowers in the spring. Some of the houses we passed were quite large. Often, four generations lived together in one home. The houses grew larger as the families multiplied. They just added more rooms.

The houses were a natural wood color, and the grounds around them were very neat. You didn't see any old cars or farm equipment lying about. The barns were close to the house or sometimes even attached. I don't know how they managed to keep them clean and odor free. All the windows were spotless.

At the top of the curvy road, we had lunch at a pretty restaurant camouflaged as a chalet. The menu was in Swiss, and consisted mostly of cheese. Our guide ordered several dishes. Of course, we were paying, and Inez grumbled that she ordered too much. The guide took a nice serving home – no doubt a way to stretch her income.

After lunch, we continued our climb. At the summit of the curvy road, we had glorious views of the Matterhorn mountain and the Eiger, both glistening in the sun.

Both on the ride up and the drive down, we saw a lot of hikers. There were singles, pairs, and whole families, wearing their lederhosen with their walking sticks, enjoying one of the first days of spring. The lederhosen are a traditional type of garment, knee length leather pants.

All too soon, it was time to leave Switzerland. I went to the front desk to check out, and our bill was huge! Our trip was prepaid, including the rooms. It took me half an hour to convince the clerk that I only owed him for a few incidentals. This was not the only time this happened. Every hotel on our trip tried the same trick.

Our guide drove us back to the airport. We were afraid we were late, due to the time change. We were acting hurried when we approached Customs. There are two things you don't do in such a situation – don't try to hurry the Customs agent, and don't make jokes.

The Customs official was very stern and didn't believe me when I told him how little money I had, (about $300), but he finally let me pass. Then he demanded to know what Inez had in her tote bag. She said, "A bottle of gin and a cuckoo clock." That would have made everyone else smile, but not him! Finally, we were released to go on to Amsterdam.

Pilatus-Steepest cogwheel railway in the world

Lion of Lucerne

CHAPTER 8

Holland

During our stay in Amsterdam, we were booked into the Krasnapolsky Hotel only 30 minutes from the Schiphol Airport. Centrally located on the famous Dover square, it faces the Royal Palace. We had planned a quiet day of sightseeing, but traveling with Aunt Inez was always full of surprises.

We had our breakfast in the solarium called Palm Court. It was quite a large, sunny room with windows for a ceiling, and a black and white checkered tile floor. Lots of flowers and palms surrounded the white tables and gold chairs where we ate. A beautiful place to start the day!

Our guide, John, was full of fun. He was one quarter Indonesian and three quarters Dutch. I'm sure you remember that at one time there was a colony in Indonesia known as the Dutch East Indies. John kept up a lively chatter as we went to the Rembrandt Museum. There we saw the famous painting, "Night Watch," and many others.

Later, we met John's girlfriend who was traveling with her own group, and she said she wanted to guide *us* – she'd heard that we were so much fun. That's how we found out that the guide from each country would tip off the next ones about what type of tourists to expect!

We toured the government buildings at The Hague and the next stop was gorgeous. The Keukenhof Gardens were where tulip growers could rent a plot and raise their most beautiful varieties.

After we toured the gardens, we ate lunch in a quaint cafe where there were Oriental rugs on the tabletops – quite unusual. We had a glass of wine and Aunt Inez became a little giddy. But she was always that way when she had a man's attention. I didn't know she had taken some antibiotics for a bothersome tooth. She was getting really wound up when we arrived at the next spot on our trip, the diamond factory.

Inside, the employees gave us a tour. First, they demonstrated the cutting process. I hoped that Inez wouldn't make a sound while they were working. The diamond cutters cut with a tiny chisel and hammer, and one slip could easily mean the difference between a priceless gem and worthless fragments. Luckily, she behaved herself.

Then we went into the showroom. It was a quiet, dimly lit place and there was some music playing in the background. The finished diamond rings were displayed on tables covered with deep blue velvet. Little spotlights picked up the radiance of the gems. Attractive young men and ladies pointed out the color and clarity of the diamonds. The whole experience was quite hypnotizing.

While we were admiring the display, we were given a little explanation about diamonds. They are formed in the liquid center of the earth. The molten material erupts, bringing them closer to the surface. Thirty percent of them are used for jewelry.

It takes a week to cut a four-carat diamond. A brilliant cut has 58 facets, an emerald cut 48, and a baguette 25. It takes 2 days to polish a diamond.

We had not gone to the diamond factory with any intention of buying. I was content with my wedding rings, and Inez preferred opals. However, one ring caught her attention. It had a curved design made up of pear-shaped stones with smaller stones filling in the curves. It fit her perfectly.

She flashed the ring around and said, "Shall I buy it?"

I didn't know what to say. I also didn't know that she had $3000 stashed on her body. Inez became louder and more excited. "Shall I buy it? Shall I fall for it?"

I was about to tell her to think it over, when she said, "You know, all my jewelry comes to you."

I'm no dummy. Immediately I yelled, "Buy it! Buy it!"

By then, everyone in the room was laughing. And on the way home, our guides bought us an armload of tulips to celebrate such a fun day.

I remember another trip, which I took with my youngest grandson when he was 14. I had signed up for an excursion to see windmills and cheesemaking. When the guy didn't have enough people for the trip, he would combine our tour group with another one.

That's how we ended up in the red-light district of Amsterdam. The Dutch have a unique way of handling prostitution. The prostitutes are confined to one area and carefully monitored. Each girl, in various stages of undress, poses in a large window so the men can stop and pick out the one they want.

This was a place where I wasn't inclined to linger. My grandson grabbed my arm and hurried me down the street to where the bus was parked. After he put me on the bus, he proceeded to give the driver heck for taking his grandmother to that place! He didn't know that I had already seen the district with Aunt Inez. But I thought it was gallant of him to defend me anyway.

We were so lucky to be there in Amsterdam around Easter. The tulips and hyacinths bloomed at the same time that year, acres and acres of flowers as far as you could see. On the way back, we stopped at a flower auction house. Men would present a large bouquet of flowers to the crowd for bidding. If no one bid on the bouquet, it was destroyed right there! Most of the flowers sold.

We thoroughly enjoyed our drive to Marken, a village in the northern part of Holland. There, we were invited to a private home. It was small, but very neat. It seemed to be built mostly in stages, with some beautiful wooden carved chests. The homes in the country all had barns attached to the houses. Thanks to this architecture, the locals could stay indoors from October to April. Everything was spotlessly clean and odor-free, as it was in Switzerland.

While we were there, we learned about some interesting customs. If a boy liked a girl, he climbed into her bedroom window, and if she got pregnant, they got married. If adults did the same, they were driven through the town in disgrace.

Coming back through the old city, John told us that house fronts were sold by the foot and were very expensive. Homes were built up instead of being built wide. Most were made of brick from river mud, and were around four stories high. There were large hooks on the roof to help move furniture in and out of the windows. Many windows also had rearview mirrors, so you could spy on your neighbors! Everywhere, Dutch housewives were vigorously cleaning windows. It was a national obsession!

We enjoyed a very pleasant motor launch ride down the canals. Seeing the river houses from that perspective was quite a treat!

No trip to Holland would be complete without stopping to watch some cheesemaking. The Dutch are famous for their cheese. We were offered a bewildering variety to choose from, and we took some back to the hotel.

Another product the Dutch are famous for is Delft pottery, a beautiful hand-painted tin-glazed earthenware. I've always admired it, maybe because my favorite color is blue. Our guide took us to a charming shop where I bought various souvenirs, including blue placemats which I still use on special occasions.

Too soon, it was time to leave Holland. What a beautiful country, and what friendly people live there. Cliff and John brought us an armload of flowers before we left. We didn't even mind that the airport was so huge we had to ride on the back of a golf cart with great big smiles to get to our gate.

Amsterdam

Bulb Fields

Windmill Tour

Villages of Marken and Volendam

CHAPTER 9

Returning Home

On our return to the States, I was concerned about arriving in the huge airport, but we went through the lines easily. Inez wore her new diamond, holding her passport over it. We felt great after such a comfortable trip.

The Customs officer asked, "Where have you girls been?"

We said, "We've been around the world!"

He said, "You look like you're just starting out!"

The Customs officer made us feel comfortable. We were not so sure about the pilot of the plane who would be taking us to Cleveland. As we were seated, he announced, "This is Captain Kangaroo," in a funny voice. Fortunately, the trip to Cleveland went fine, but as we came in, we noticed the wings were not level. Everyone who had a window seat was pushing up with their other hand to level them out. Thank God we landed safely.

After he picked us up, my husband complained that his back

suffered from carrying Aunt Inez's bag. We found out later that she had taken four sets of Japanese airline silverware!

At home, when my son saw me, he said, "Look at her legs!" They had become quite thin. I wonder how many miles we walked on that trip?

Aunt Inez stayed with us for six weeks, and she and I basked in the glow of all we had seen. The downside was, no one wanted to hear about it. Even my husband didn't ask a single question.

Shortly after we got back, I met a friend at the bank, and he said "Where have you been? I haven't seen you in a while.

"Around the world!" I said proudly.

"Yeah," he said, "but where are you going next year?"

Inez went home and was proud to show her slides to her friends in the local Elks Club, the ladies who were known as the Elkettes. For the next five years, she stayed well and happy in her own home. But when she came down with the shingles, I flew down to get her. She was comfortable living with us, until she passed away in 1984. We then took her ashes to her hometown of Portsmouth, Ohio, and had a nice graveside service. Her husband had been buried there since 1939! We were even able to get a marker like his!

I will always be grateful to Aunt Inez for that wonderful adventure. Not many people get to go around the world in one trip, even today.

PART II

Other Cities

CHAPTER 10

Paris

It doesn't seem right for a book about traveling around the world not to include Paris and London. But Aunt Inez thought they would be too much for her on our original trip.

After she was gone, my husband and I retired to Port St Lucie, Florida. We had a very pleasant eight years there, and then he passed away in 1996.

Before my husband passed away, I had started writing a book and this was the godsend that I used to fill my days. I joined 5 writers' groups in the area. Many of the leaders of the groups and my fellow writers were connected to various colleges in Florida, and I received a lot of learning and editing from them.

But during this time, I missed the opportunity to explore the world. I wondered how I could travel again, and then the idea came to me. Why not take each of my 5 grandsons to Europe? What a wonderful experience for them and for me! They were all well-behaved kids, and all A students. I decided to take them before they could drive, and before they were old enough to go out at night without me!

We used a company called Globus Tours, and they were wonderful. Most expenses were paid in advance and you had the protection of having a driver and a guide. It also eliminated any debate about where you were going at what time and where you would eat.

The groups traveling on these tours soon became a family. The young people gravitated to each other and formed close friendships, making it all the more fun.

Paris looked like it was supposed to, one beautiful picture after another. Broad boulevards were framed by flowering trees and attractive shops. They led to ornate traffic circles complete with statues, shrubbery, and impressive arches.

The residential areas consisted of row upon row of stone buildings, built close to the street, with a courtyard behind for parking. Parking was a problem, even with the small cars and motorcycles that most people used. They parked horizontally two and three deep in front of the apartments. This must have been quite a system to get in and out of. Many apartments looked alike, as they had been built by the same architect after a huge fire.

Nearby, the Eiffel Tower looked even bigger than it seemed in pictures, and was very impressive when it was lit up at night.

I arrived in Paris with my grandson, Rory, and a group. Rory was 14, and hadn't had a growth spurt yet. I said, "Rory, stay right with me. Your mother will kill me if anything happens to you." I would have loved to bring his mother with us on the trip, but unfortunately, she was fighting cancer.

As soon as he got off the bus, Rory was so excited, he took off running right through what looked like a flock of huge birds. Instead of birds, though, it turned out to be a team of soccer players from Africa with their wide robes flapping in the brisk wind! It was very dark, and there was nothing for me to do but stand there and wait for him to return. Soon, he came walking back with some friends from the tour, unaware of the scare he'd given me!

On my trip with Rory, enormous numbers of lights were outlined on the tower, counting down to the year 2000. On my next trip to Paris with my daughter Ruth, I was again at the Eiffel Tower at night, when a runner with an Olympic torch ran past us, climbed the tower, and rappelled down a wire to the adjourning park. This was completely unexpected and quite a thrill.

A large crowd gathered around us to watch the runner. By chance, I was in the front row. The crowd pushed me forward, and the cop was pushing me back. Ruth almost got into a fight with the policeman. He wasn't being very nice about shoving us backward, and I was frightened. As soon as the torch landed back on the ground, the crowd let up, but I never want to be in that position again. We were only across the street from our hotel, but the policeman made us go back through the park. We grumbled all the way.

The next day, we had a pleasant boat ride down the Seine, traveling under one beautiful ornate bridge after another. We arrived at the Louvre, where the big attraction was the beautiful painting by Leonardo da Vinci, the famous "Mona Lisa." A big advantage of being on a tour is that your guide knows when to see things, when the crowds are smaller. We were able to get quite close to the painting, and it was truly awe-inspiring. Of course, the Louvre holds thousands of treasures, and we enjoyed many of them during the time we had there.

I will never forget the crystal pyramid adjacent to the museum. Known as the Louvre Pyramid, it was made of glass and metal and was designed by the Chinese architect, I. M. Pei. In my opinion, it would be spectacular somewhere else, but it didn't seem to fit into the area as I saw it.

Later, we were lucky again to have a beautiful day for a trip to Versailles. The Versailles Palace is U-shaped with 1000 rooms. To me, the room plan seemed odd. The bedrooms all open on one end to a hall which runs along the outer wall. Consequently, there would be no privacy.

The reception rooms and dining rooms were ornately decorated. Jackie and John Kennedy went to the Palace Versailles on their first trip to Europe after John Kennedy became president in 1961. You could just picture Jackie Kennedy strolling down the famous Hall of Mirrors. What a privilege to be there – just glorious.

Outside, the gardens went on as far as you could see. At one time they covered 7000 acres!

Two smaller, adjacent palaces were built nearby for transportation, one for the horses and one for the carriages. Known as the Gallery of Coaches in The Great Stables, they held small carriages used for entertaining Marie Antoinette's children. They entertained every Monday, Wednesday and Thursday night.

Back at the hotel, we were hot and tired, and Rory was not impressed with the menu in the restaurant. The waitress understood perfectly. She sat us at a little table by ourselves and brought him a pizza.

Nearby, on a big screen TV, soccer finals were going on. That was all Rory needed. The finals went on every evening during our trip and were a godsend to keep the younger ones entertained!

The next day, we had a chance to shop at a nice department store. We chose some fabric for Rory's mother, who was a talented dressmaker. The clerk was friendly and very helpful in figuring out the yardage, etc.

For dinner that night, we went to a lovely restaurant on a busy corner of one of Paris's famous traffic circles. As we sat eating, the cars sped around and around, honking their horns and jockeying for position to exit. I found it very dizzying, and not the best thing to watch while eating.

On another trip, with my grandson, Ryan, when he was 17, I signed up for a nightclub tour to Moulin Rouge. The famous place advertised a steak dinner, wine, and a floor show. Everything was great. The show featured topless dancing girls. They were small and shapely and skipped quite quickly across the stage. In the restaurant, they were very generous with the wine. I was a little giddy going back to the hotel.

One of the mothers in our group said to me, "You didn't take Ryan to that show, did you?"

Ryan answered, "Yes, but it was tastefully done!"

The next evening, we went to Montmartre, a hill on the Right Bank of Paris that is 430 feet high and famous as the site of the Basilica of the <u>Sacré-Coeur</u>. To get to this high point, with the cathedral on top, you go up by a funicular, which is like a small elevator. The site is an artist colony, and for some reason, I didn't feel comfortable there. I asked a couple from our group if Rory and I could stick with them.

There were a lot of illegal Hindus in the area with trinkets to sell. They would spread them out on a cloth about the size of a card table. The cloth had strings on all four corners that could be snatched up in a second if a cop appeared, and boy, those guys could run!

Later, we had a nice dinner "al fresco" and I was just as happy to head back to the hotel.

I was sorry to leave Paris, but was excited to see London. We had a long bus ride to get to the hovercraft, an amphibious boat which would take us across the English Channel. The hovercraft uses air below the hull to move the boat along. We watched it arrive and drive right up to a cement ramp. Then it heaved a great sigh, expelled all its air, and its passengers disembarked.

A Globus representative escorted us onto the craft. The seats were as fine as in the best tour buses. When we were ready to leave, the beast inhaled lots of air, and we rose several feet. Then the boat went in a circle, and headed into the English Channel. It's a fast way to cross to England, but it is noisy and bumpy.

One thrill that repeats each trip is seeing the "White Cliffs of Dover." As we passed them, the famous song from World War II was running through everyone's mind, and quite a few people on the boat were humming it.

Hall of Mirrors

Montmartre – Paris Artist Quarter

Palace of Versailles

Ryan and Arlene In Paris

CHAPTER 11

England

I wasn't impressed with my first look at London. On our way from the airport, we drove through a low rent district. The houses were a mishmash of architecture. Many had storefronts on the street level. Most were empty.

We soon came to better neighborhoods, and were surprised to find that we were staying in a Hilton. It had a gorgeous lobby and wonderful service. I must say that our travel agency, Globus, outdid the international travel agency Trafalgar as far as the quality and locations of our hotels.

That evening we took a cruise on the Thames River to see the lights come on in the city. We passed the magnificent Houses of Parliament. Again, Globus had impeccable timing; we passed Big Ben at exactly 9:00 p.m., when the bells rang out. What a memory!

The next day, we walked past the apartment of Prince Charles, to see Buckingham Palace. We weren't allowed too close, so we strolled the outer grounds, and then went back to curbside to see the changing of the guard.

A procession of well-kept black horses went by, with their riders resplendent in red uniforms and high beaver hats. A band followed in similar uniforms, coming straight at us from their barracks. They turned at the corner. Rory was there with his camera. He would never have a better look at the changing of the guard!

What a treat to see Westminster Abbey! This English gothic cathedral has been the site of almost every British Coronation since 1066, and the venue for many important weddings.

Next, we went to see the chapel of Henry the VIII, built in 1503. This was one of the most beautiful chapels in Europe. The nearby poets' corner honored Chaucer, Thomas Hardy, Tennyson, Browning, and others with monuments and tombs.

Sir Christopher Wren, an architect who was also an astronomer and a mathematician, created the 17th century masterpiece, Saint Paul's Cathedral. Other churches have been on the same site since the year 604. The Cathedral's chief purpose was to be the center of worship for the City of London, for the nation, and for the world. Its music, architecture, and liturgy, are famous.

While in London, we learned an important fact about traveling with a group. One couple was habitually late. On the trip to Saint Paul's, evidently the driver and guide ran out of patience, and at the appointed time, we left the couple at the cathedral, and went back to the hotel. I never did hear what the cab ride cost them.

One other site that was impressive was an enormous Ferris wheel on the banks of the Thames River. While it was beautiful, especially when lit up at night, it didn't fit into my notion of London, with the view of the Tower Bridge and Parliament.

William the Conqueror built the Tower of London in the 11th century. This was a favorite stop for my grandsons, due to our fantastic guide. He was dressed in a full Beefeater outfit. The elaborately dressed Beefeaters were considered Her Majesty's guards. Our guide knew all the facts about the Tower of London, and had a great sense of humor.

The new Jewel House in London displayed the vast collection of priceless Crown Jewels. These included state gold and silverware used during centuries of Coronation ceremonies. We saw the 530 carat Cullinan diamond, known as the "Star of Africa," and Queen Victoria's Crown, studded with 3000 jewels, mostly diamonds.

The dark side of the tour was the Execution Room where Anne Boleyn, second wife to Henry the VIII, met her fate. Over the course of history, many others were also executed there.

Of course, a few days is not enough to see London. But we enjoyed the bus rides between tours when the guide would point out places we had heard of over the years, Piccadilly Circus, *Trafalgar Square,* and even Harrod's Department Store.

Before we knew it, it was time to head for home via Heathrow Airport. The airport was under construction (aren't they always?). We followed the arrows and walked and walked. Finally, we ended up in about the same place. We had walked around the entire building!

Home at last! When we arrived in the United States, we were met by our family members. One of my other grandsons said of Rory, "I could see a change in him when he left the plane. The trip really helped him grow up."

Arlene and Roy in London

Beefeaters of London

Buckingham Palace – Pomp and Ceremony

Flowers Near Big Ben

Forum – Roy – 6-98

Roy Sketching at the Forum

CHAPTER 12

Rome

I didn't want to leave Rome off my travel itinerary, but it wasn't included in my trip around the world with Aunt Inez. We couldn't see everything we wanted during that journey and she was more interested in Switzerland and Holland.

I did take my two oldest grandsons, Ryan and Rory, on the Grand Tour of Europe, which included Italy.

As for the other three grandchildren, Dan toured Italy with his father. I took Keith and Kyle and their parents on a trip, which included Italy. I found that much less tiring than the long bus rides, easier and more enjoyable.

The first time we traveled to Rome, we were booked into the Michelangelo Hotel, (miracle of miracles), which was only a 5-minute walk to the Vatican and near the Arno River. We were greeted by our guide, "Ali," who had a wicked Dutch accent. She told us to go right into the orientation meeting which had already started. From there, we went to dinner in the same clothes we had worn all day! The restaurant was noisy, but after a good meal of chicken and vegetables, complimentary wine, and three loud musicians, we began to relax.

After a good night's sleep, we were up early to stand in line at the Sistine Chapel. This was the only way to avoid crowds. While we waited for half an hour, a local guide gave a talk in the middle of the square. Then there was a long walk through the Vatican Museum, lined with precious art and elaborate ceilings. At last, we arrived at the Sistine Chapel, which has been beautifully restored with lavish use of orange and green.

As you may know, the center dome of the Chapel shows God creating Adam. They are reaching out their arms to each other, but their fingers don't touch. Michelangelo was probably telling us that we should be closer to God. It was too much beauty to take in. I found I could not look up and walk at the same time. It was hard to take in the amazing art around us with the groups moving forward.

Saint Peter's Square is lined on both sides by a huge colonnade which leads to the facade of Saint Peter's Basilica, the center of world Catholicism. Saint Peter, one of the 12 apostles of Jesus, was crucified by the emperor Nero on this spot. In 324, the Emperor Constantine ordered a basilica to be built there in his honor. This building holds so many treasures, it's hard to grasp. Michelangelo designed the dome, and the building also contains his famous sculpture, the Pietà.

The Pietà shows the body of Jesus sprawled across the lap of his mother Mary after his crucifixion. When I was in Rome at that time, the Pietà was on display somewhere else, but I did have the thrill of seeing it later at a New York City World's Fair. Its beauty is extraordinary. Gazing at it, you are in awe of how a man could create such a masterpiece.

On another trip, Rory and I ended our tour of the church and the Chapel about 11:30 on a Sunday morning. We found some steps facing the square, shaded by a balustrade. There were only a few tourists about, and it felt good to sit and rest for a bit. We both knew we were praying for his mother, who was at home dealing with stage four cancer.

The Pope was due to appear at a window in his apartment at noon. I wondered where the crowd was. Shortly before noon, the vast place filled up with people. Buses unloaded swarms of tourists. Everyone was cheering, "Viva la Pope!"

Soon, the crowd hushed as the Pope appeared before them and spoke for a few minutes. Then the cheering started again. I am a Protestant, but I felt very moved by the whole scene, and had tears in my eyes.

The crowd seemed to melt away as quickly as it came. Rory and I had a beautiful walk back to the hotel along the Arno River. We talked to some young people there who were selling crafts. After we got home, Rory painted a large oil painting of the Arno, which I still cherish.

During our trip, we had some short stops. For example, anyone who goes to Italy has to toss coins into the Trevi fountain, which was completed in 1762. The fanciful fountain features Neptune standing on a chariot pulled by winged steeds. We were there after dark, and it was magical.

And then there was the Colosseum. It could hold 50,000 spectators. We think of the Colosseum as being large, and it was – in its day. For example, where I went to school, Ohio State University, the stadium could hold over 80,000 people! The Colosseum was started in AD 72 by Vespucci. We've all seen movies about the bloody battles held in the Colosseum between men and between animals and men. What I didn't know was that it could also be flooded and display battles between ships!

Time and weather have taken a toll on the Colosseum, and there is just a shell remaining. There are three tiers of columns left, Doric, Ionic, and Corinthian.

As we drove along, I was greatly impressed with how the builders saved every small piece of antiquity. If they are laying a sidewalk, they will save a piece right in the cement. If a wall goes up where a pillar stands, they include it as an art piece in the wall. New buildings are designed to blend in with the old, using used bricks, etc.

I had expected Rome and Paris and London to be modernized and to lose their individuality, but the opposite was true. Each one clung fiercely to their special charm. What a wonderful opportunity! We stayed in the best hotels, and had wonderful meals. Back then, everything wasn't crowded with tourists like it is today. The year 1974 was a wonderful time to go around the world. The famous golfer, Arnold

Palmer, was flying around the world at the same time, but unfortunately, our paths didn't cross.

One afternoon, we drove to the Tripoli gardens, a choice summer resort since Roman times. It was a gorgeous park on a hill with a beautiful valley and mountains in all directions. At the top was the *Villa Adriana*, where Lucrezia Borgia, an infamous Italian noblewoman, once lived.

Walking downhill was easy, but coming back up was a real workout. There were some graded slopes and steps, and at the end, there were two steep staircases that led back to the Palace. My advice is, get in some training before going to Tripoli gardens.

Next, we drove to an even higher slope to eat at a restaurant. What wonderful views of the city we saw in that restaurant, just as the lights were coming on. Our waiters gave us appetizers, and wine and champagne before, during, and after dinner.

At that time, Italian men were known to pinch the bottoms of visiting women, and savvy lady tourists wore girdles. While I was eating dinner, I heard odd little squeals, and I'm sure some of that was going on.

Five musicians played up a storm while we ate, and a couple of tenors sang their hearts out. One was barrel-chested, and looked like Pavarotti. Between songs, this musician played a wooden clapper in time to the music. He handed it to Rory and my grandson played along for quite a while.

By then, we were all feeling no pain, and we were sorry to see the evening end. As we boarded the bus, there was Rome below in all its glory.

Arlene on the way to Florence – 80th Birthday

Firenze – Italian for Florence

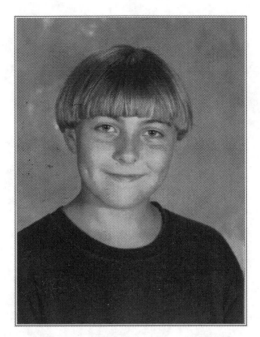

Grandson Dan

Grandson Keith

Kyle Arlene Keith

Leaning Tower of Pisa

Michelangelo's David

Roman Forum

Ruth Kyle Keith Arlene Jim

St. Peter's Square – Rome

The Colosseum – Interior

Vatican Museum - Rome

CHAPTER 13

Venice

Rome was fantastic, but the side trips were also amazing. I had always dreamed of seeing Venice. From what I'd heard, it seemed like the most romantic place ever.

Well, as we found out, it is spectacular. The Grand Canal is huge, and fascinating architecture arises on the shore. At the entrance to Saint Marks Plaza is the Basilica de San Marco. It is the third church built on this site, and dates from the 11th century. It is one of the most ornately decorated Catholic churches, with Byzantine mosaics covering the ceilings.

Behind the altar is the Palo del Oro screen with the sarcophagus of Saint Mark in front of it. The screen is one of Saint Mark's greatest treasures, with over 2000 precious stones.

Saint Marks Square is the center of Venice. It's surrounded by shops, cafes, and colonnades. While we were there, a small orchestra played, and numerous pigeons scattered around. There were groups of chairs here and there, but no one was sitting on them. I later learned that you have to pay to sit there.

While we were standing in line to go into Saint Mark's Basilica, we were informed that no one was allowed in wearing shorts. That didn't bother the guy in front of me. He slipped off his shorts, pulled a pair of jeans out of his backpack, and slipped them on. It all happened in a second – amazing sleight of hand.

It had rained before our visit, and there were big puddles all over the square. The local workers put boards over the puddles to assist those walking in the area. In a little department store, the water was two inches deep on the ground floor. We have always worried about Venice. It's been sinking for years. With the rising water problem now, I don't know what will happen to it!

A gondola ride has always been on my "wish list." I didn't care if it was expensive and a touristy thing to do – I was going for it. The evening couldn't have been more perfect. Our poler, the man who manipulated our gondola through the canals, didn't sing, but one on a nearby boat did. It was magical to glide down the smaller side canals and see the lights come on in the city. Sure would like to do that again.

Of course, there is much more to Venice than the canals and Saint Mark's. Near Saint Marks is the Campanile, an Italian bell tower. This was the tallest structure in Venice. After it originally collapsed in 1902, it was rebuilt in the 20th century.

Venice also has many museums, the largest of which is the Gallerie del'Accademia in Northern Italy. It has the largest collection of Venetian artists in the world, including Vittore Carpaccio, Giovanni Bellini, Giovanni and Titian.

Nearby is the Peggy Guggenheim museum. This museum contains the world's greatest collection of modern art. It is housed in a palazzo that originated in 1750, that was once her home. Guggenheim's walls display works by Pollock, Ernst, Chagall, etc. A sculpture garden contains work by Giacometti, Mirko, and Falkenstein.

The Venetians are also famous for their blown glass. We had a tour of a workshop where it is made. It's just amazing how intricate some of the work is. While it was very interesting, I was glad to escape the "blowing" room, as it was very hot. The display rooms had shelf after shelf of beautiful objects for sale. I'm sorry now that I didn't buy anything, but it all looked so fragile, I was afraid to ship it home.

Someday, I would love to go back to Venice. It is unbelievably beautiful and interesting.

Venice – Sunset on St. Mark's Bay

Venice – Basilica San Marco

CHAPTER 14

Pompeii

In 79 AD, Mount Vesuvius spewed a cloud of ash and rocks 12 miles into the sky. Wind blew it south, and it fell on Pompeii. Like a heavy snow, it collapsed ceilings, while leaving many walls standing.

Most of Pompeii's 20,000 residents had fled when the volcano started to erupt, but the last 2000 citizens were caught in the next hot flow. They were all buried under 30 feet of volcanic ash. The city's location remained a mystery for 1500 years, because the volcano filled up the harbor, changing the coastline.

Pompeii was rediscovered in 1599 during construction, and serious digs began in 1748. They are still going on. Archaeologists were able to make plaster casts of some who died, and even reconfigured a horse all saddled up. Glimpses of everyday life, such as bakeries, drinking fountains, and bars and bordellos were discovered. They even found a set of loaded dice.

Colorful frescoes on marble plaster walls displayed the opulence in which the citizens of Pompeii originally lived. Founded in 600 BC, it was a port city. What a pleasure it was to see it.

CHAPTER 15

Florence

As we continued our trip, on our way to Florence, I had a great beach day on the Riviera. I would have liked to spend more time there, and I especially wanted to see Monaco. Maybe sometime in the future.

It was also great fun to view the Leaning Tower of Pisa after seeing pictures of it all those years. The tower stood by itself in a field, which was kept nicely mowed and trimmed. There were no distractions like snack bars or T-shirt shops. A former ploy by tourists was to stand some distance away and pose so it looked like you were holding up the Tower.

Florence is a wonderful city in which to tour museums and churches. The Bargello Museum was first built in 1255 as a fortress. It houses priceless sculptures by Michelangelo, Donatello, and Cellini. It also includes ivory sculpture, medieval weaponry, frescoes, and porcelain.

Nearby, the huge Church of Santa Croce was built between 1294 and 1442. While it holds an extensive collection of treasures, it is more famous for being the final resting place for various famous Florentines such as Michelangelo, Rossini, Machiavelli, and Italian composer Antonio Salieri.

The most famous attraction in Florence is the Galleria del Academia. The statue of David, sculpted between 1501 Anne 1504, stood in the Piazza della Signoria for four centuries until it was transferred to the Galleria to protect it. The statue was considered too precious to be outdoors at the mercy of tourists and the weather. A copy of the famous statue now stands outdoors in its place in the Piazza della Signoria.

During our visit we had a fun side trip to the Leather Guild and Gold Market. Italy is famous for its fine quality leather goods. There was a beautiful display of handbags, jackets, and smaller items.

One attractive young lady with our group had her hair piled up under a baseball cap. Our handsome clerk wanted her to take it off. She finally did let down a beautiful cascade of sun-tinted hair. He was delighted, and slipped an expensive leather jacket on her. She looked like a million bucks, and we all smiled and clapped.

This short piece doesn't do Florence justice. There were so many more places to see. The whole city is full of treasures and history. I like to think one's first trip to Europe should be on a guided tour. Then later, you could go back to the places you enjoyed the most and spend more time there.

For me, Florence would be one of those places.

PART III

China

CHAPTER 16

China

I awoke in a cold sweat – anxiety attack. The door through the wall of Communism that surrounded China was slowly opening. And I was going in. The plane would land soon. What had I let myself in for?

How did I end up on this trip? I'd heard about dental groups going to China in a dental publication. I thought it might be interesting so in 1984, I made an application as a hygienist, and was issued an invitation and a visa by the China Association of Science and Technology (CAST).

CAST was an organization of 106 Chinese scientific organizations under the leadership of the Communist Party designed to promote science and technology. The main task of CAST was to organize academic exchanges. I was now one of a group of 11 hygienists and four dentists under their direction and protection for three weeks.

It was dusk as we circled to land. There didn't seem to be many lights below. The fresh October air felt wonderful as I left the plane.

Funny, I had flown a third of the way around the world, and the weather was the same. Akron, Ohio, and Beijing are all at the same latitude!

The terminal was very large and new looking, and we were soon lined up to go through Customs. We had been told to be very patient. According to what we were told, the little men who held these jobs were very "self-important," and they liked to delay you for any excuse.

I was concerned, because I had no luggage to inspect. Mine had been lost before I arrived in San Francisco. I was almost to the gate when my bags suddenly appeared beside me. Very mysterious, these Orientals!

I then had to explain what was in my 3 boxes of supplies. The customs officials had no idea what dental floss was, so I whipped out a piece to demonstrate. The people waiting in line behind me were not amused.

We were met at the airport by two CAST guides who would be with us throughout the entire trip. The young man, Mr. Nu, didn't look like a typical Chinese person. His face was more angular. He wasn't overloaded with personality. He seemed preoccupied and cross, like he was just putting up with us. The other guide, a young lady named Miss Wu, was a doll. She had a sweet round face, and she smiled all the time. She didn't wear Chinese clothes, but had tailored slacks and blouses that fit her perfect figure. I can still hear her lyrical voice saying, "This way."

We were loaded on a comfortable new bus, and we started through the semi-dark streets. Everything seemed to be one color – drab. We passed blocks and blocks of cement apartment buildings. Each apartment had one window, and we could see one bare light bulb hanging in the middle of the room for light. The streets were empty of cars, and only a few pedestrians were seen hurrying home.

The depressing scene fit my mood. We were heading for the Longevity House, the walled compound where President Richard Nixon had once stayed. Ordinarily, I would have been excited about reliving that important moment in history. However, a woman who had been there earlier told me to watch out for rats. When I asked her how big the rats were, she said, "If you think you see a cat, don't pet it!"

I had wanted to stay downtown on **Tiananmen Square.** One historic hotel there was where foreign correspondents stayed, and it had a view of the Square and the Forbidden City. You may be wondering why I didn't stay where I chose to stay. It's very simple. You stay where the Communist Party decides you should stay. You go and see what the Communist Party wants you to see, and you stay with your group . . . period. Come to think of it, you also eat what they want you to eat. We were never given menus.

We passed through the gates to the place where we were staying. There was an armed guard in a small sentry box on each side. It was dark now, and the place looked like a scene out of a Halloween movie. A large brick courtyard led to a portico with pillars fronting a large dark stone building.

The lobby was dimly lit, and was furnished with worn, overstuffed chairs. We were given our room keys and the luggage was put in a heap in the hall. There was one serious hitch. One of the doctors had packed his high blood pressure medicine in one of his supply boxes instead of carrying it with him. One of the girls accidentally had the box with her stuff. They searched everywhere for that medicine. They looked in the airport, the bus, and so forth. The doctor's health was seriously endangered until that medicine was found three days later.

My hotel room was furnished with heavy, dark furniture and velvet drapes, almost Victorian in style. A thermos of hot water for tea and a thermos of drinking water were kept filled. We soon learned to stay dressed at all times, as the hotel clerks could walk in at any time to complete the refills.

The hotel bathroom had an open sewer running under the floor. I put a paper basket over the hole, but it was always back in the vestibule whenever I returned to the room. The girls in the next room told us not to try to keep any secrets. When I opened the medicine cabinet in the bathroom, I could see through to the next room. A lizard was kept in the crevice by the tub in case any insects walked by.

As soon as we put down our things, we were called to the dining room for dinner. The Chinese had attempted to brighten it up with some small lights and tinsel. It looked exactly like a club room on the day after New Year's Eve.

The meals were served at round tables for eight. You did not pull up extra chairs, or take any away, because each course was put in the center of the table and contained exactly 8 servings. The food did not even resemble what is served in Chinese restaurants in the states.

For example, one large fish was served. Each person helped themselves to a serving (about one large teaspoon full) and that was eaten before the next course was served. Those in the party with a boardinghouse reach had the advantage over me with my short arms. I had to stand up to reach my food.

Like I said, after the fish there might be a bowl of broccoli, then some small pork ribs, a bowl of rice, tofu, bok choy, shrimp, and so forth. No bread is served, and you had your choice of orange pop or beer to drink.

It was actually very safe to eat the food, as it is cooked over high heat, and also our hosts would "lose face" if we became ill. The food was nicely flavored, and it was a lot of fun wondering what the next course would be. There was very little duplication in the menus.

I was beginning to know the group a little better. Our leader was a tall, attractive blonde from Minneapolis. She had led a group before, and was a tremendous help. She sent us pages and pages of "do's" and "don'ts," and lists of things to take with us when we were preparing for the trip. It was very obvious later that some know-it-alls didn't read the instructions. They made some serious blunders which I will tell you about as we go along.

The group was from all over the country. One doctor from Nevada seemed to be more than an acquaintance of our "glorious leader." There were two black lady doctors from Chicago. One hygienist was an ex professional ice skater. My first glimpse of her was on the plane. To get from her window seat to the aisle, she walked on the armrests, so she wouldn't disturb her seatmates.

One hygienist from New Orleans brought her banker boyfriend with her. He turned out to be a great help in deciphering the money. We also sought his help when making any major purchases. I was surprised that they roomed together, as we were told the Chinese were very prudish, and didn't like any hanky-panky in their hotels. Maybe they didn't realize the two weren't married, because in China, a woman keeps her maiden name.

My roommate, Mavis, was from Philadelphia. She was so happy to be on this great adventure. Her husband had, without previous clues, left her for another woman. Her elderly parents were ill and she was having serious trouble with her teenagers. She left all that behind and was an enthusiastic traveler.

There were also three people who taught at a University in Kentucky, a dentist, his wife and another woman. It was soon apparent that this was a "triangle," as they say. Old proverb, "There are three things you can't hide, smoke, love, and a man riding on a camel." Well well.

One of my earlier fears had been that we would work all the time and not get to see the sights. So, I was happy to hear that a trip to the Great Wall was scheduled for the very next morning.

Arlene Lawless with Chinese Children

Arlene at Sacred Way China – 1984

Arlene at the Great Wall – 1984

With Doctor and Nurse

CHAPTER 17

The Great Wall

The day I had anticipated had finally arrived! We were going to the Great Wall of China. There are many things in China that can spoil your plans – road slides, political unrest, snowstorms or sandstorms – but that day was all clear.

After a breakfast of egg rolls, scrambled eggs, toast and coffee, we boarded our bus for the 48-mile trip to Badaling. There was a familiar squeak squeak squeaking sound from the back seats. One of my fellow hygienists had bought long balloons to shape into animals. She and the other smokers sat in the back and made those animals on the long bus rides. They were a big hit with the children at all our stops, and some help to me. Whenever I became too engrossed in my travels, and lost my group, I could always follow a trail of little children with balloons.

The road out of Beijing was very straight for a while, and was lined with trees that looked fairly new. They were two and three feet deep along the sides and some were in the median strip. Each citizen of

Beijing was required to plant 2 trees a year to replace the ones that had been chopped down for firewood.

Before they were ousted from power, the "Gang of Four," a political group formed by four Communist Chinese party officials, had a really stupid idea. They decided to kill all the birds because they were eating grain in the fields. Killing the birds made the insect problem worse, so they dug up the grass to get rid of the insects. And that brought on dust storms. So, they had to admit they were wrong, and eventually they reversed the whole process.

After a while, we stopped at a cloisonné factory. Cloisonné is an ancient art that uses metallic pieces or wires to create shapes that are then decorated with glass, various gemstones, and other objects. The factory was in a small wooden building out in the countryside, and the girls there were making beautiful jewelry. The bus drivers made time to stop so we could make purchases. I wouldn't be surprised if the drivers got a cut of the sales, as they were always very upset when we delayed them and they missed a store.

Stopping at this little store was also a chance to go to the latrine, and I do mean latrine. That situation was also very bad at the Great Wall, Tiananmen Square, and even in the nicest restaurants. We soon learned to carry our dental masks with us, and the Chinese girls would laugh at us as we stood in line wearing them.

On the way to the Great Wall, we stopped at the Sacred Way. This path was originally known as "the road to heaven," a road the emperors would use to return to the heavens after death. It was built in 1540, to be used only by royalty on their way to the Ming Tombs. A hush came over our group as we passed under three marble arches, and then went through the Great Red Gate. Here, we entered the "Avenue of the Animals." A huge stone tortoise was at the entrance, the symbol of "long life." Life-sized statues of lions, camels, horses, elephants, and two sets of mythical beasts lined the narrow roadway, followed by 12 statues of military men who guarded their emperor.

I walked slowly along the path, absorbing every detail. I let the group drift ahead of me, as I didn't want to be distracted by chit-chat.

I wanted to fall under the spell of that ancient civilization and culture. It worked too well – I still haven't recovered.

At the end of the road a man was selling trinkets, and I bought a few. He told me in pretty good English that he appreciated our visit and that our purchases helped the local people. I gave him a toothbrush, and he gave me a watercolor his son had done of the Great Wall. Quite a nice cultural exchange, one that would have been unheard of a few years earlier.

At last, we came to the Great Wall. I was prepared for its height, 21 feet, but its width surprised me. It was 18 feet wide to accommodate 5 cavalrymen or 10 infantrymen. The part of the wall open to tourists was very steep. I had trained at home by walking a mile or two up and down a hill every day, but now I wished I had done more. I was also glad that I had good walking shoes, because the stones were worn round and slippery. I did see some tourists in high heels! I was taking my time going up to make sure I made it to the top, when a little old Chinese grandmother went sailing past me. She must have had legs of steel.

The group had scattered during the climb, and I found myself alone at the top. I was glad to be able to savor that moment, to hear only the sound of the wind blowing through the parapets. The view was breathtaking. Looking north toward the Gobi Desert, I could imagine the hordes approaching on horseback. Looking east and west, it appeared the wall went on to infinity, rising and falling with the grid lines of the hills. A total of 300,000 men had labored the length of 3000 miles to build the wall. Many were buried inside it when they collapsed from overwork. All of that was in vain, for the enemy could breach the wall easily by bribing the sentries.

How wonderful it was to be there and experience that history. It was a highlight of my life.

The descent was tougher than going up. The stones seemed even more slippery on the way down. A young Chinese couple took my arm to assist me. They also sold me an embroidered and appliqued vest. They wanted to give me Renminbi in change. Renminbi is old Chinese money, and you may not carry it out of the country. Instead, I asked for yuan and they agreed.

Arlene Lawless

At the bottom of the wall, I saw a beggar sitting on the ground. He was laboriously taking apart a cardboard box to retrieve a little piece of foil. I circled him, trying to get a good picture. Then I noticed an armed guard circling me. The Chinese do not want you to take unflattering pictures of their country, and they will confiscate your camera and your film. I retreated, and sauntered off to the gift shop to buy a sweatshirt that said, "I climbed the Great Wall."

CHAPTER 18

After the Great Wall

While traveling around China, I found that the bus rides were just as fascinating as the stops. On the way up to the Great Wall, I saw a few men and women working to widen the road. They were chipping away at a cliff of solid rock, with only a pick, a shovel, and horse-drawn cart to work with. On the way back, I saw that they were working by the light of a single lantern.

We stopped for dinner at the Ding Ling restaurant. I had to chuckle at that one. It was named after one of the emperors buried in the Ming Tombs. Nowadays, I imagine we would have trouble paying respect to a leader named Ding Ling.

We were served duck, asparagus, fish, rice, sponge cakes, shrimp, Bok choy, egg drop soup, and 100-year-old eggs. The 100-year-old eggs tasted suspiciously like plain hard-boiled eggs to me.

There was a large gift shop attached to the restaurant where we started our first shopping frenzy. Who could resist silk blouses or silk nightgowns for $4, silk ties for $1, and other great bargains in ceramics and artwork?

Back at the hotel, we had a toothpaste sorting party. Our leader brought 3000 rejects from a toothbrush factory at home, and we picked out the usable ones to give away to clinics and schools.

During this period of time, I couldn't help but notice the progression of our "love triangle." The forbidden ones were giving each other long looks across the crowded room, while the wife coped by getting drunk. She must have brought a supply of alcohol from home because there were very few bars in China.

One night, the wife decided to lead us in song while we worked. She chose the Stephen Foster song *Way Down Upon the Suwannee River.* I didn't think that was a great idea because two of the members of our delegation were black, and the song *Suwannee River* has a reputation for being rather racist. But the wife waved off my suggestion to sing another song. She stood in the middle of the room, singing loudly and waving her arms to direct us to sing along. When we came to the line, "Oh, darkies, how my heart grows weary," she stopped dead, realizing how she had blundered. There was an awkward silence, and then our minds all clicked in at once, and we hummed the line and finished the song. Our black colleagues laughed heartily at our discomfort, and we laughed with them.

The next day, we visited a commune on the outskirts of the city. There the residents grew vegetables for Beijing. The cabbages and onions were huge, and one of the girls in our group asked me why they were so large. I told her they used human manure, and she said, "I wish you hadn't told me that!"

We all felt that this was a model commune, a show for tourists. As part of the tour, a man named Mr. Jung gave us the statistics about the place. A commune is about the size of a county in the United States. This one had 45,000 people and 1300 acres in crops. Income per person was $800 per year. He said they had 58 tractors, but I didn't see any. In fact, I didn't see a tractor the whole time I was in China. The commune also had one hospital and three dentists.

A retired couple showed us their living quarters. I'm sure it was a job assigned to them, and they weren't happy about it. They acted afraid of us, and were very reluctant to have their picture taken. They thought the camera would steal their soul.

The homes were all one story, attached to each other, and surrounding a courtyard. I was surprised to see that the one we toured was furnished with blonde wood furniture, a style popular in the United States in the 1950s. They were proud to show us that they had electricity (1 bare bulb hanging from the ceiling), and running water, which meant a pump in the middle of the courtyard. We smiled and thanked our hosts for the tour, but they never changed their stoic expressions.

We stopped in the childcare center to teach the children about tooth brushing, but they were way ahead of us. Each child had a cup and a toothbrush, and they showed us how to brush!

The little ones stayed all week in the childcare center so their parents could concentrate on work. The rows of tiny beds and the wall of small washcloths on hooks brought a tear to my eyes. This wasn't the way I was raised. How lonely they must be at night, I thought. They did look well-fed and well-cared for though, and their beautiful round faces just beamed at our attention.

When we went on the factory tour, it also looked staged. In one enormous room, a few women were cutting and sewing clothes. They had some on a rack for sale, and I wanted to buy an item from them as a goodwill gesture. But the materials were very rough and cheap looking, and there was no style to them at all.

On our way back to the hotel, we stopped at the zoo to see the pandas. They were smaller than I expected, about half the size of our brown bears. But they were very beautiful, striking in their black and white fur. It was late afternoon, and there was only one patch of sunlight near them. I was trying to get a good picture when one of them read my mind. He picked up a carrot, wobbled over, and sat in the patch of sun to pose for me!

CHAPTER 19

Beijing's Academic Exchange

The next day, we were to have our first Academic Exchange at the Beijing Stomatological Hospital at 9:00 AM. We found that the Chinese are very specific about timing. When they say, "Be on the bus at 8:30," they *mean* be on the bus at 8:30. If you are late, they will leave you. The Chinese doctors and other dignitaries were always lined up on the steps every morning to greet us, so it wouldn't do to be late.

I approached the hospital with some fear and trembling. Our leader had cautioned us that there might be sights, sounds, and smells that we were not used to. For instance, they used carbolic acid to disinfect everything, and this has a rather putrid odor. We were told to keep a pleasant and professional expression on our faces no matter what.

Dr. Wey and Dr. Li Pu Ching lead us to a reception room filled with comfortable, overstuffed chairs and small tables with crocheted doilies for "tea and briefing." This little custom was repeated at the start of all our "exchanges." The doctors were quite pleasant as they gave us a tour. This hospital was the oldest stomatology hospital in China. All the dentistry in Beijing was done there. In other words, there were no private practices. The hospital had a staff of 590, and over 1000 patients. There was room for 50 to stay overnight and six divisions available for outpatients.

As we continued our tour of the different departments – immunology, pathology, and the research laboratories – we noticed that the cleaning personnel were not keeping up with cleaning the floors and stairways. Plumbing dripped everywhere. Remember, this was 1984, and the Chinese were not used to today's standard of building. Even the newest hotels had peeling wallpaper and water drips. The joke was, "What is the national bird of China?" and the answer was, "The building crane." We saw those cranes everywhere, but none of them seemed to be working.

The library in the hospital was shockingly small. The "Gang of Four," which had reined during a previous decade, had burned most of the books. Their idea was to get people back to the farms, and to prevent them from learning. It would take years for the Chinese people to make up for that lost time.

After our tour, we returned to the conference room, and two of our members gave presentations. Margie demonstrated how to sharpen instruments. She put her arms around a Chinese girl, guiding her hands, to show her how to sharpen the instruments. This immediately became a photo op, with the Chinese gathering around her.

Next, Kathy gave a presentation on sealants, which was well received. We gave the attendees many gifts of toothbrushes, floss, and books.

Lunch was at the Lai-Jin Yu Xuan Restaurant. We had an appetizer plate that consisted of tomato wedges, tofu, and mushrooms. Then we were served cauliflower, creamy scrambled eggs, spicy fish, dumplings with a plum center, rice, shrimp, apples in spun sugar, soda pop and beer. The restaurant was near the entrance to the Forbidden City, and we eagerly looked forward to our afternoon tour.

CHAPTER 20

Forbidden City

What a thrill to get a tour of the "Forbidden City!" Dating from the Ming dynasty in the 15th Century, the forbidden city was the home and workplace for the Chinese emperor's entourage, family, officials, workmen and servants. For 500 years, until the fall of the Qing dynasty in 1911, the city was off-limits to commoners. Occupying over 183 acres and surrounded by a 35-foot wall and a moat, it really *is* a city.

Many emperors and servants never left its protection. They believed they were at the center of the universe. There are six palaces in the City with 9,000 rooms. If a leader felt they were in danger, they would sleep in a different room every night.

Walking from the front gate to the back takes half a day. The palaces are several yards apart through the center. The courtyards were all paved and steps and ramps leading up to the palaces were reserved for certain classes of people. Some of the ramps were used strictly for carrying the Emperors.

The palaces were mostly shells of their former selves. There were some battle instruments, large jars, embroidered robes and furniture, but much of the treasure once held in the City had been looted through the years. The living quarters, bedrooms, dining rooms, etc., were along each side. Our tour took half a day. I don't know how long it would have taken if we also went to visit the side buildings.

The City was opened to the Chinese in 1949 when the People's Republic of China was formed. On the day we were there, many Chinese tourists, couples and families were enjoying the sights and the beautiful day. The City is so enormous, I can't imagine it ever being crowded.

The same is true of Tiananmen Square, which the Forbidden City faces, and which is the center of Beijing. Very large government buildings surround the square, one of which houses the embalmed body of Mao Zedong, the founding father of the People's Republic of China. There is always a line outside that building to view him.

The weather smiled on us again the next day when we visited the Summer Palace outside the city. This palace was very ornate, with the roofs containing tucked-up corners. The palace is on a lovely lake, and at the water's edge sits a marble boat. During the 1800s, there was some discussion about building a navy. The dowager empress demonstrated her power by putting her money into that marble boat, instead! We wonder how that changed the course of history. It certainly kept China isolated much longer.

After dinner, we walked under an elaborately decorated archway along the lake, to our bus. The rich red and gold colors of the archway gleamed in the fading sunlight, and sand glittered in the air as the moon rose. We walked slowly along, trying to absorb all the beauty. I was thinking, "I'm walking where the Dowager Empress walked. I am looking at the same moon!"

It was one of the most enchanting moments of my life.

Xian was our next stop. As we assembled to get on the bus to the airport, I noticed a large crowd of Chinese Commoners filing into the auditorium behind us. They looked so bored and tired. There was no smiling or chit-chat like that in our group. No doubt they walked there, or rode bicycles or busses to get there. Then they had to listen to a big pep talk about Communistic propaganda. I felt so sorry for them.

As for our group, we eagerly looked forward to our next trip, seeing Xian and the famous archeologic excavation.

CHAPTER 21

Xian

Beijing fascinated me, but I felt a sense of relief when we were on our way to Xian. Beijing is the center of the government, and I always felt under the strict control of the Communist Party while there. I happily left that dreary hotel.

At the airport, we stood in line for a long time. Due to our over-enthusiastic buying, our luggage was overweight and we each had to chip in an extra ten dollars before we could board our flight. The banker and his friend in our party were asked to have their luggage checked through separately since they were the big spenders in the group. At the next stop, we gave away even more toothbrushes and books, so we came out better with the weight.

Once we arrived in Xian, I couldn't believe my eyes. The hotel, also built by the Russians, was a duplicate of the one we had just left – big, dark and gloomy!

We first reported to work at a Military Hospital. I anticipated stern fanatical military types who would intimidate us, and I was worried. Was I off track! The military doctors who greeted us on the front steps were very young and had big smiles on their faces. But it was hard not to laugh at them. They were standing there in the most ill-fitting uniforms you can imagine. I was reminded of a song from an operetta about the "ill-assorted Guard." Their sleeves hung over their hands or were too short. The shoulders didn't come close to fitting and the pants were of all lengths. In fact, they looked like they were playing dress-up in their Dad's old uniforms.

The reason they were so friendly was that Americans had put up the money for that hospital, and they were very grateful.

Since we were here, it was finally my turn to demonstrate how to clean teeth. The doctors brought in a young man to be my patient, and he looked terrified. Back then, many Chinese had never even seen an American, and you can imagine this young man's fears as a blonde, blue-eyed American girl put her hands in his mouth.

I smiled and tried to look pleasant and harmless. Wouldn't you know it, he had a calcium deposit on his teeth like cement, and a lot of it! In addition, I was working with equipment like I started out with in 1948 – not only that, but I'm left-handed. I did the best I could in the short time that had been allowed for us. When the young man left, he still had the look of terror on his face. I was glad to have that duty fulfilled. Now I could relax and enjoy the rest of the trip.

As we came out and went on our bus to various other trips, the Chinese people were smiling and friendly. It was not considered rude to stand and stare at strangers. They were like children, just interested in what you were doing. In one shop, they crowded around watching what CDs I would buy. I like to think I may have made a star out of some unknown singer.

The highlight of our trip to Xian was the visit to the Qin Shi Huang excavation site. This was the tomb of China's first emperor. The day started out bright and sunny and we were all excited about seeing this most significant archeological find. Initially, peasants digging a well in 1974 uncovered a terracotta warrior and called authorities. Further investigation uncovered 6,400 figures buried over three and a half acres. The warriors plus horses were guarding the tomb of Qin Shi Huand Di, the emperor of China from 221 to 210 B.C. He was the emperor who unified China and finished the Great Wall.

A dome covers an area the size of a football field and you walk on catwalks to view the scene. The front of the life-sized statues were restored and stand in rows. Behind them, many were still not excavated. It was an eerie sight – a face might be looking up or an arm would be reaching up out of the dirt. It was a haunting place, with body parts all over. How tragic that so many man hours and resources were spent on guarding a dead emperor! Even more tragic, all those with knowledge of the sight were also put to death so that it would be a secret forever. The plan almost succeeded.

The trip back to town that day was a nightmare. The bus driver seemed to be in a big hurry. The road was narrow and very dark. Hundreds of bicyclists were coming towards us on their way home from work. The driver would turn on his headlights for an instant to get his bearings and then turn them off again so he wouldn't blind the cyclists. In between flashes of light, he drove with his horn.

I was cold, scared and exhausted, but I had a little Scotch in my tote bag for just such emergencies. I asked the dentist sitting next to me if he wanted a little Scotch. He said, "Is the Pope Catholic?"

After breakfast the next morning, our leader, Jan, called me aside for a private talk. The message was grim. She had received a wire from her family in the United States saying that her mother had died. When she left on her trip, her mother was very ill and was being cared for by her sister and her teenaged children. She had told them not to contact her in China if her mother passed away because she knew she wouldn't be able to do anything about it. But they sent her the wire anyway.

When she got the wire, Mavis wailed and sobbed. We put our arms around her, and we all cried. Her ailing mother had promised to hang on until Mavis returned, and her family had promised not to send her any bad news while she was so far from home. She felt doubly betrayed. As her family was Jewish, the burial would be the next day, and she couldn't get home for the funeral. She decided to finish the tour. Throughout the day, each member of the group expressed their sympathy for her.

We went on to visit the Pan Po excavation, which was 7,000 years old. Xian goes back 8,000 years. No wonder the Chinese resent it when we young'uns from our State Department try to tell them how to run their country.

Two huge towers stand on the outskirts of the city. One had an enormous bell and the other had drums. Sentries posted on top would send signals by way of the bell and drums to alert the people when invaders were approaching. I could imagine the terror in the peasants' hearts when those sounds echoed all around them.

The Chinese know little about construction. We saw them putting up brick walls without mortar. They were also in need of good plumbers and electricians.

By gesturing with my camera, I asked a Chinese gentleman who was sitting on a stool in the courtyard if I could take his picture. He had long white hair and a long white beard, and he was wearing glasses. It's unusual to see eyeglasses in China. He made a striking picture with the sun glittering off the gold rims. He posed willingly and after the shot was taken, he jumped up and vigorously shook my hand. He wasn't as old as he looked.

I heard an unusual sound coming from across the street, and I went to investigate. Three men had a little storefront business, carving tombstones with only a hammer and a chisel. After a pause, one would start chipping, another would start, then the third. The unusual aspect of this was that they played in a cadence which was musical. I'm sure their day was less tedious that way, and it was quite pleasant for anyone who had to listen to it.

The day grew very dark and cold. Smog was settling in. There were no restrictions on smokestacks at this time, and we could see large particles of soot in the air. When this soot combined with the fog and sand blowing in from the Mongolian Dessert, the situation was miserable.

After dinner, a few of us went to inspect the hotel's new bar that had been set up as a favor for the tourists. It was a regular hotel room with the beds removed and an old-looking bar placed across one corner. On it were a few bottles and some grungy glasses. Three tables that each seated four people were covered with rumpled tablecloths. A few Chinese men were in the room as we entered, but they left immediately. I think they were afraid to socialize with us.

I took one look at those dirty glasses and decided to return to my room. Our "romer" doctor offered to escort me back across the large dark courtyard. He left his wife with the others in the bar, and I was sure he was using me as an excuse to get to his girlfriend. I was grateful for his protection though. Even though we had been assured we were very safe in China, foreigners were considered guests and crimes against tourists were very rare.

As we crossed the courtyard, the smog was much worse, and I felt like I couldn't breathe. We were to fly to Guilin the next morning, but there had been a report that the visibility was so poor, the airport was closed. I prayed it would clear up by morning. I felt like I would die if I had to stay in Xian another day.

When I returned to my room, my roommate, Mavis, was asleep with her mask on! I got very tired and quickly got into my bed. I was about to fall asleep when Mavis woke up and decided to call a masseur. She was very tense over her mother's death, and thought a massage would help. Our guide, Mr. Nu, brought a young man who looked suspiciously like the "doctor" one of our party had called earlier for a sore foot. I think he would have been called a "Jack of all trades" in the states.

Mr. Nu told Mavis that she couldn't be nude for the massage, so she put on a gorgeous pink satin slip. Mr. Nu sat in a chair in the corner. I don't know if he was there officially or just curious. I think that was probably the sexiest thing he had ever witnessed – halfway through the massage, he bolted from the room.

As he was leaving, a Chinese man with a big, buck-toothed grin stuck his head in and asked me if I wanted a massage. "No thank you," I said in a quavering voice, and I pulled the covers up higher under my chin.

CHAPTER 22

Xian to Guilin

The next morning was sunny and clear, thank God. All traces of the terrible smog were gone and the airport was open. The waiting area looked like an old train station, with wooden benches – like old church pews – provided for seating. In an attempt to cheer up the place, lengths of bright blue yard goods were tacked alongside the tall windows to resemble drapes. The results were hideous. I felt such sympathy for my roommate. It was obvious that Mavis had been crying again, and she was sitting there all dressed in black on that long hard bench. A more forlorn picture you couldn't imagine.

The Chinese knew exactly who we were, what we were doing, and what we had purchased, but the petty bureaucrats delayed us for as long as they dared. We heard that the further away from Beijing you traveled, the lighter the Communist grip, so we were happy to be on our way to Guilin. Going from Beijing to Guilin is like going from Maine to

Florida, and we were looking forward to warmer weather – although it was coming a little late. We had all developed a cough.

When we arrived in Guilin, we boarded a bus with our regular guides and a new guide for that area. His name was Mr. Ford, and he had a terrible overbite and had trouble talking over his large teeth. He announced that Guilin had a beautiful new hotel, and went on and on about its various attributes.

My roommate looked at me and said, "Well, it's about time, after the gloomy places they have put us!"

Mr. Ford continued bragging about the new hotel as we drove by it. And then he said, in all innocence, "But you're not staying there!" Mavis and I laughed until we were almost hysterical, and only straightened up after our leader gave us a stern look.

The hotel we were assigned to was very nice. The lobby walls were covered with bright mosaic tile pictures of flowers and palm trees. It had a cheery dining room and a lovely atrium filled with flowers, shrubs, fountains and large fish sculptures. Our morale definitely improved.

As soon as we put our bags in our rooms, we were whisked off to a local department store. I wanted some tapes to go with a slideshow about China that I was planning to create. (I did get some great pictures and presented various slide shows to friends and families when I got home. These programs were well-received.)

The clerk spoke some English, and with a little effort, I chose one vocal and one instrumental arrangement. A large crowd of Chinese citizens gathered around me to see what I was buying. They stood wide-eyed, like children, staring unabashedly. There was nothing threatening about this. They were just curious, and after a few days in China, you get used to it.

I had become so absorbed in the shopping, I was late for the return bus. I dashed out to the parking lot, which was full of buses just like ours. Frantically I ran from one to another, knowing that the drivers always left right on the dot. The reality of the situation hit me. Our stop at the hotel had been so brief, I didn't even bother to write down the name of it. In addition, I had just spent the last of my money. I remember thinking to myself, as I ran from bus to bus, "I will never, ever make these mistakes again!"

Finally, in the last lane almost to the highway, I spotted a bus with balloons on it! My bus. When they realized I wasn't on board, the group had yelled for the driver to stop I can't imagine what would have happened if I'd missed that bus, and been stranded in a strange city with no money. You can bet my heart pounded for a while after that close call.

CHAPTER 23

Guilin

I awoke the next morning to the sound of roosters crowing in the yard below the hotel window. The sun was rising over the Li River. What a beautiful sight as the light fog gradually lifted. Iridescent green butterflies wafted in the open window, heralding the enchanting day awaiting me.

We were going to take a boat ride down the picturesque river. The pointed mountains that lined its banks are often featured in Chinese paintings. I was thrilled to be on my way to see them.

The bus took us to the dock. The area was packed with people and the driver couldn't park very close. We had to run the gauntlet, weaving in and out of the way of other tourists and resisting various vendors who reached out to us and called to us to buy their trinkets.

There wasn't much dockage space, so the pilots simply tied on to a boat already there and ran planks from one deck to another. It was quite an adventure hurrying from one boat to another, trying to find Boat

Number 3. Once aboard, we were fed the usual multiple course lunch, and we were on our way.

Parts of the river were very shallow, so our boat was towed by a smaller one. It was wonderful to glide along with no engine noise or vibrations. Our pilots had to be very skillful to maneuver us through the shallows and around the rocks and rapids.

The Li River and the Karst formations that lined its banks were a stunning sight. The formations are pointed as a result of erosion from an uplifted seabed 300 million years ago. The karsts are covered with emerald green foliage and have been the inspiration for artists down through the ages. Some of the karsts had distinctive shapes and had descriptive names such as, "Elephant Trunk Hill, "Old Man Peak," and "Nine Horn Hill," for example.

In between the peaks, on the banks of the river, there were tiny settlements consisting of simple wooden houses and plots of rice, sugar cane, and bamboo. Water buffalo worked the fields and bathed in the river. Little children frolicked at the water's edge, calling, "Allo, allo," as we glided by. Their laughter echoed across the water when we tossed them candy and then toothbrushes. Trained cormorants, tethered to bamboo rafts, caught fish for their masters. We saw whole families living on small sampans, the small, flat-bottomed boats native to that area. Every moment was a photo opportunity of a lifetime and I had to remind myself to sit quietly and enjoy one of the most beautiful sights on earth.

The trip of 31 miles took six hours – talk about a slow boat to China! But every minute was sheer delight, and it ended too soon, at Yanshuo, where the bus met us.

On the way back to the hotel, we made a brief stop on a rise in a farming area to admire the golden rice fields ready for harvest. The gorgeous and prosperous-looking area left me totally unprepared for what happened next.

A group of small children approached us. They were dirty and looked like they didn't have enough to eat. I had some balloons, and tried to hand them out one at a time. One little boy snatched them all and soon they were all grabbing at me with little skinny hands like claws, clutching at my purse and my clothes. Their desperation saddened me and frightened me at the same time. I struggled to get through the small crowd of children and back to the bus. Once aboard, I could give them money by making them reach out one at a time. Those sad little faces will haunt me forever.

Arriving back at the hotel, I realized the date was November 6, election day in the United States. I asked at the desk and I asked passersby if they knew the results of the election. No one seemed to know, but they did know the score of a Chinese girls' volleyball game that had been played that day in America.

The few people that I've talked to about the election were positive that Reagan would win. And they were also sure that Reagan intended to make war on China. Although it's a bad idea to talk politics in China, I assured them that Reagan didn't want war and everything would be okay. So much for my diplomatic experience.

At the hotel, all the girls made a beeline for the hotel beauty shop. I let our leader, Jan, go ahead of me as she had long, thick hair that took longer to dry. By the time that was decided, all the beauty operators were taken and a barber in the connecting barber shop offered to do my hair. He put the shampoo on and worked the lather for several minutes. I didn't know if that was their method or whether I should tell him when to stop. He also rubbed my forehead, neck, and temples. Later I found out that a head massage is a regular part of a shampoo in China.

While my shampoo was being completed, another hygienist let the barber at the next chair do her hair. She asked for a full massage. She remained in the chair, fully dressed, and he rubbed her arms and legs. The next day, they were bruised all over.

When the barber started to set my hair in rollers, he looked very bewildered. I kept still as he put a big curler with a clamp in the middle of my forehead. I knew the clamp would leave a big crease in the wave, but I didn't want to correct him and cause him to "lose face." He then put me under an ancient hair dryer that made horrible noises. At that point, I wasn't worried about style. I was just hoping my hair would dry before I was electrocuted.

Even at that, I fared better than my friend, Jan. We were all at the dinner table and she arrived late. It was her birthday, and we had a cake and gifts for her, and were eager to get on with the festivities. She arrived in tears. The girls had rolled her hair in brush rollers. After the hair had dried and she tried to unwind them, they became hopelessly tangled and she had to cut chunks out of her hair to set herself free!

Jan was a good sport, however, and after some wine and cake and lovely gifts, she was back to her usual cheery self.

CHAPTER 24

Guilin to Guangzhou

Before our flight to Guangzhou the next morning, we had time for a ride along the Pearl Flower River to the Reed Flute Cave. The Cave is the most famous in China, and gets its name from the reeds at its entrance. The reeds are used to make flutes, and they are also used to conceal the entrance. Long ago, peasants hid in the cave to escape from wars and bandits.

Inside, there were magnificent stalactites and stalagmites. Some were lighted by colored spotlights to enhance their beauty. A 160-foot path wound through the cave and then suddenly opened up into a vast grotto known as the Crystal Palace. This grotto can hold 1000 people, and it is an awe-inspiring sight.

We were served tea at the airport, and soon boarded a plane for our one-hour flight to Canton, now called Guangzhou. Guangzhou has long been an important shipping and trading center, much of it conducted by the British. The architecture of the city reflects that influence.

Our first duty was to visit a school to teach toothbrushing. Some of the students and teachers were out on the steps to greet us when we arrived. They had a program all ready for our visit, and again, we felt this was a "model" prepared for tourists.

First, they performed some exercises to Chinese music out in the school yard. When we went into the auditorium, the pupils filed in holding cups and toothbrushes, and they sang a little song, demonstrating that they knew all about tooth brushing. So, I didn't have to do any work that day. A musical program followed, with singers, dancers, violinists, and pianists, all very talented.

The principle was a sturdy, no nonsense type of woman. The children were so well behaved, I asked her if there were ever any discipline problems. "Only with beginners," she replied. I believed her.

This was our last city in China, and we just had time to see the Sun Yat-Sen Memorial Hall before our farewell banquet. Sun Yat-Sen was the leader who overthrew the imperial form of government in 1911. The round theater, which could seat 5000, had a stunning blue glazed tile roof, and there were no pillars inside to block the view of the stage.

We were honored to have vice chairman, Mr. Shan, and secretary general, Mr. Lee, of the China Association of Science and Technology at our farewell dinner. Also present were a new junior diplomat from the United States to China, and his wife. This was a formal banquet, with 23 toasts! I could tell our diplomats were new. One drink of the distinctive Chinese drink known as the Maotai and his face was beet red, while the wife gamely tried to eat a chicken wing with chopsticks!

The menu for our celebratory dinner included ham with pineapple, mushrooms, duck, shrimp, sliced beef, bamboo shoots, broccoli, sweet and sour pork, crab claws, egg drop soup, chicken and peanuts, Jelly cookies and almond soup. The waitress then brought tea and hot towels, and finally, we left.

There was a message at the hotel when we arrived. We had left before the meal was over. They were greatly insulted, and we probably wouldn't be invited back there again!

CHAPTER 25

Guangzhou (Canton) to Hong Kong

At the train station the next morning, we had to rush to get our money changed before boarding. The cars that were sent for us were air conditioned and beautifully decorated. They had lace curtains, and blue velvet drapes graced the windows. The reclining seats would turn 180 degrees, so you could enjoy the view out the window or talk to the person behind you.

The bad news was that, when it came to the trains, there was only one rail line. Our train was not as important as freight trains, so when a train came from the opposite direction, we were shunted off onto a siding to wait for it to pass. The 75-mile trip took six hours. I had carried granola bars with me all through China in case of delays, but I'd given them away at our last stop. The dining car was packed with people, so I went hungry that day.

I did get two memorable photos on this trip. At one stop, Tantuxia, a group of women were dressed in peasant costumes, long black dresses and black sun hats with black fringe. They contrasted sharply with the white, sunlit wall of the station, and made a striking picture.

Another shot will be indelibly etched in my mind. A man in full harness, like a horse, was pulling a truck load of scrap paper. He even had a strap across his forehead. His body was at a 45-degree angle from the pavement and he was clearly straining to keep pulling. This was not an unusual sight in China. Men also toiled along the riverbanks, pulling boats upstream that way.

Another heartbreaking sight was a sign beside a river which read, "Do not drown baby girls here." This was a sign that resulted from a law created in China In 1980 to help reduce China's overpopulation problem. One of the tragic repercussions of the "one child per family law" was that couples who had a baby girl first would murder her so they could have a boy. They believed that a boy would provide for them better in their old age than a girl. Another backlash from this policy of having mostly boys came when the young men grew up. There was a serious shortage of wives. Sometimes, North Korean girls were smuggled in, but if they were caught, they were returned to their own countries.

Our group would be leaving China soon, heading across the border into Hong Kong. I was a little worried. I had heard that the border guards were afraid to get too close to the line, and you had to drag your bags across yourself. I also heard they could give you a rough time checking your stuff. Imagine my shock when I looked in my purse and found that the moneychanger had given me Renminbi folded up inside other money. Why in the world would he do that? It was strictly forbidden to carry old Chinese money out of the country, and there I was, not far from the border. My first thought was to tear it up and flush it, but we were stopped at the moment, and it would probably have fallen down onto the tracks. I was relieved when one of the doctors walked by and took it off my hands. I don't know what he did with it, but he didn't get caught.

All that worry was for nothing. Our Hong Kong guide eased us through the border with no difficulty, and we had a smooth bus ride through the New Territories to Hong Kong.

CHAPTER 26

Hong Kong

In Hong Kong, you can get a suit made in three days. Our guide immediately rushed us to his favorite tailor. Ultrasuede was very popular then, and all the girls were eager to get fitted.

I didn't go for this, though, because I didn't like being rushed. And anyway, my daughter at home was an excellent dressmaker and made many of my clothes. The guys checked and found that the tailor at our hotel was actually less expensive.

We checked into the beautiful Royal Garden Hotel. Everywhere you looked, the walls and doors in the lobby were made of Lalique glass. Very modern, clean and attractive. The cultural shock was huge. We had just spent three weeks in an agrarian country, 50 years behind the times!

Mavis took off like a shot for the stores, but I just had to relax and decompress. I felt like I had been in outer space.

The beautiful dining room was in one section of the lobby. Strangely, I was very hungry for tuna salad. Luckily, they had a tuna salad sandwich, and I had one for three days in a row. There was a McDonald's nearby, and some of the group rushed over. But no way was I going to travel 8000 miles to eat at McDonald's!

When Mavis returned, we both went out shopping. One shop after another contained attractive bargains. I bought some beautiful silk fabric for myself and my daughter. At home after my trip, she made each of us a lovely dress. My print had small birds on it, and she hand made a wooden belt buckle with a bird painted on it.

But that day in Hong Kong, Mavis and I bought some jewelry, various saki sets, and gifts to take home. Silk scarves were a good choice, as we always had to keep weight in mind. I asked Mavis to walk to the Peninsula Hotel with me. I wanted to relive my stay there in 1974 with Aunt Inez.

The hotel was still considered the Grand Dame of hotels, and was closely protected. Almost immediately a security guard started watching us. When we lingered a little, he asked what we were doing there. I told him I had been there in 1974 and just wanted to reminisce for a few minutes. He was not a bit encouraging, and Mavis was anxious to get going, so we left.

Later, we "shopped till we dropped" and went back to the hotel to change. The entire group met at a nearby restaurant for dinner, which turned into a lively talk fest. Everyone was thrilled with the adventure we had experienced, and they congratulated our guide for the excellent job she did.

The next morning at the airport, everyone was coughing. The pollution was bad everywhere, but not as bad as it was in Xian. I have always wanted to go back to the Orient, but nowadays, with the profusion of cars there, the air is much worse.

Upon boarding the plane, we found it half empty. I was able to grab three seats in the center section and lie down in them. I slept all the way across the Pacific! Was I lucky!

Going through Seattle for Customs was very easy. I was soon on my way to Akron, Ohio and my family. What an unforgettable experience that trip was, and memories for a lifetime!

EPILOGUE

I am writing this book at a terrible time in our nation's history. I have plenty of time to write, as I am quarantined due to the pandemic of the COVID-19 virus. I live in an independent senior's apartment where my meals are delivered daily. We have a beautifully maintained campus of 100 acres where we can walk freely. We must wear a mask when we are close to people. The social life has come to a screeching halt.

Another big worry is the riots going on in major cities. Large gatherings of any kind are causing the rapid spread of the virus. But I am fortunate to be in a safe place with dear friends. Thanks to the vigilance of our management, we have had only two cases of the virus out of 600 people.

I pray our country's problems will subside soon, and we will find a revived appreciation for America.

BIO

Arlene Lawless was born in Marion, Ohio and enjoyed a small-town childhood. She graduated from Ohio State University with a degree in psychology and is a Registered Dental Hygenist (ROH) in Dental Hygiene.

Arlene married David Lawless, a Firestone man, and had three children. After retiring to Florida and becoming a widow, she started writing, traveling, and performing stand-up comedy.

Her previous books are, "Breach of Promise Letters," (https://www.amazon.com/Breach-Promise-Letters-Arlene-Lawless/dp/0595185789/) and "Bo doesn't live here anymore."

Printed in the United States
by Baker & Taylor Publisher Services